THE
TRUTH ABOUT
DRACULA

THE
TRUTH ABOUT
DRACULA

GABRIEL RONAY

STEIN AND DAY/*Publishers*/New York

First published in 1972
Copyright © 1972 by Gabriel Ronay as *The Dracula Myth*
Library of Congress Catalog Card No. 72-83095
All rights reserved
Printed in the United States of America
Stein and Day/*Publishers*/Scarborough House, Briarcliff Manor, N.Y. 10510
ISBN 0-8128-1524-6

THIRD PRINTING, 1973

Contents

A section of illustrations appears between pages 86 and 87

Acknowledgements

The author gratefully acknowledges the valuable assistance extended to him by the following people and organisations: British Museum Library; National Szechenyi Library, Budapest; Professor Dr Roswitha Wisniewski of the Germanistisches Seminar of Heidelberg University; Professor Paul Anton Keller of Graz; Professor Ya. S. Lurye of the Russian Literary Institute of the Soviet Academy of Sciences, Leningrad; Sir Ian Moncreiffe of that Ilk; and those who preferred not to be mentioned by name.

The map of Hungary is reproduced by courtesy of the British Museum.

The author's thanks are also due for permission to quote from the following books: *Beowulf*, translated by David Wright, © David Wright 1967, published by Penguin Books Ltd; *The Prince* by Niccolo Machiavelli, translated by Luigi Ricci, revised by E. R. P. Vincent and published by Oxford University Press, reprinted here by permission of the publisher.

Preface

Generations of readers the world over have accepted Bram Stoker's vampire 'Dracula' as gospel. Many more to come, no doubt, will read the story of the Transylvanian vampire and never question its accuracy.

Attracted by a baffling feminine -a ending in the name, I found myself digging deeper and trying to ascertain whether the vampire Dracula tradition had any basis in fact or was merely a bogy sprung from the imagination of the last real writer of Gothic romances.

The feminine -a in Dracula proved to be a red herring, but a critical analysis of historical facts has helped to identify without a shadow of doubt the historical Dracula as Vlad the Impaler, a fifteenth-century ruler of Walachia. He was guilty of many unspeakable and horrifying deeds but vampirism was not one of them. For that the blame must be placed on a sixteenth-century high-society lady with a castle in the foothills of the Carpathians; the female of the species is more deadly than the male.

The Countess Elisabeth Báthory, the only reliably recorded vampire in the annals of Europe, used the blood of virgin maidens to stave off old age and retain her beauty. Bram Stoker's fiction is no match for this real life horror. Although the cruelties of Vlad the Impaler shocked and fascinated Renaissance Europe and became a legend already in his lifetime, they pale beside the hair-raising deeds of the Vampire Lady.

The roots of the vampire tradition and the pagan blood healing lores, so manifestly present in Countess Elizabeth's acts go deep and penetrate to the very core of European culture.

Statesmen, the churches and a multitude of ideologies have

made through the centuries a great use of the vampire tradition. In more enlightened times the Dracula myth owes its survival to man's inability to accept death. The promise of an *alternative existence*, be it on the simple level of Bram Stoker's un-dead Dracula, or the Faustian quest to conquer eternity, is implicit in it.

This book traces the fate of those who have helped to keep the Dracula myth alive, and examines the reasons why belief in un-dead vampires will live on long after the demise of the ideologies and religious teachings which exploited it to suit temporary aims.

PART ONE

ONE

Of Vampires Ancient and Modern

A vampire, according to the *Oxford Dictionary*, is 'a ghost (usu. of wizard, heretic, criminal, etc.) that leaves his grave at night and sucks the blood of sleeping persons'. It derives from the Hungarian word *vámpir*.

The vampire tradition, however, was widespread and well established in Europe even before the Hungarians lent their apt word to this baffling phenomenon. There were blood-sucking, evil ghosts in the lore of ancient Greece and Rome. The Greeks knew them by the name of *lamiae*, the Romans called them *striges*, *mormos* or *lamiae*. Their definition of the activities of these ghostly creatures was fairly vague, but they were believed to be 'un-dead' persons who return from the grave to prey on or devour the living under specific conditions.

Euripides and Aristophanes referred to the *lamiae* as 'pernicious monsters', while Horace* alluded to the prevalent belief that these vampires devoured children alive or sucked their blood until they expired. Ovid asserted that *striges* were vampires capable of assuming the form of ravenous birds 'which fly about at night sucking the blood of children and devouring their bodies'.

Louis Lavater, a sixteenth-century Protestant theologian who made a thorough study of the vampire phenomenon, compiled a fairly comprehensive list of the un-dead creatures in which the classical world had believed.†

'Mormo', he wrote, 'is a female form of hideous appearance, a

---

* Horace in his *Ars Poetica* writes: 'Neu pransae lamiae vivum puerum extrabat alvo'.

† Louis Lavater: *De Spectris, Lemuribus et magnis atque insolilis Fragoribus*, Geneva, 1575 edition.

Lamia; sometimes considered to be the same as Larua . . . Lamiae were thought by ancient writers to be women who had the horrid power of removing their eyes, or else a kind of demon or ghost. These would appear under the guise of lovely court-esans who, by their enticing wiles, would draw some plump rosy-cheeked youth into their embraces and then devour him wholemeal.

'Lamiae are also called Striges. They are birds of ill-omen, which suck the blood of children lying in their cradles, hence the name is also given to witches whom Festus (the Grammarian) terms sorceresses or uolatice.'

A legend that grew around Polycrites of Thermon, governor of Aetolia, has the basic traits of certain types of vampire occur-rences—the returning of the dead from the grave and the de-vouring of a human being as an omen of calamity—in ancient Greece. He returned from his grave, 'pale and ghastly to see, clad in a black robe blotched and splattered with blood, as his wife and young infant were being put to death by a mob. On seeing that the mob was bent on burning his wife and child on a stake, he suddenly seized the child and tore it to pieces with his teeth.'

The panic-stricken people of Thermon saw the ghost of Polycrites swallow huge chunks of the child's flesh until only the head was left intact. Then, to the amazement of the crowd, the child's head spoke, foretelling (rightly, as it turned out) the de-feat of the Aetolian army. Although not the type of vampire that one would associate with the blood-suckers of post-Christian Europe, Polycrites was, to all intents and purposes, an un-dead crea-ture returning from the grave.

Phlegon of Tralles, the freedman of Hadrian, recorded another type of vampire occurrence, which also lacked blood-sucking but reflected the boundless sensualism of the un-dead—one of the main attributes of female vampires.

Phlegon's story relates the case of a young girl, Philinnion, who returned from the grave to spend amorous nights with Machates, a young man living in her parents' home. The girl was dis-covered, some six months after her funeral, in bed in Machates' room. Night after night she was seen through a crack in the door by her old nanny, making love to the young visitor. Eventually she told her mistress of Philinnion's unfettered love-making, but the girl's mother would not believe her.

After some questioning, however, Machates confessed to the family that he had indeed been sharing his bed with an amorous ghost, and she had presented him with a golden ring and a ribbon as a token of her love. The parents recognised the ring and the ribbon immediately—Philinnion had been buried with them.

The following night when the re-animated body of Philinnion appeared at the usual hour in the young man's bed the parents burst in on the couple and fondly embraced their long-missed daughter. But instead of giving an explanation, the un-dead girl told her parents: 'Oh my mother and father dear, cruel indeed have you been in that you grudge my visiting a guest in my own home for three days and doing no harm to anyone. But you will grieve sorely on account of your meddlesome curiosity. For presently I must return again to the place that is appointed for me. Do also learn that assuredly it was not contrary to the will of God that I came hither.'

With that she fell back dead in the bed in which minutes earlier her pliant limbs had embraced her lover. The family vault was immediately searched but Philinnion's coffin was empty. There was, however, in the coffin a ring that the young man had given his amorous visitor as a love-pledge. On the instructions of the city elders Philinnion's body was burnt on a pyre outside the city walls.

A type of female vampire that used the pleasures of love-making to ensnare handsome youths and drain them of blood and devour them, was greatly feared in ancient Greece. Philostratus in his *Life of Apollonius* describes a classic case of erotic vampirism, revealing the sources of the belief in this particular species of the *genus vampiricus*: man's primordial sexual fear of the woman who initiates and then devours (castrates) the young male as she receives him.*

* Sir James Frazer noted in *The Golden Bough* that among savage tribes it is still customary for lads at puberty to undergo certain initiatory rites, of which the pretence of killing the boy and bringing him to life again is the commonest.

The story contains all the symbols and archetypes of Virgil's *Golden Bough*, with the scene of the strange tragedy transposed from the secret grove in a sylvan landscape to the bedroom of an ancient Greek town-dweller. Menipus, a friend of Apollonius, is young and handsome like a pagan god, while the priestess of love is disguised as a courtesan and stranger to the Greek shores.

'Menipus was supposed by most people to be loved by a foreign woman, who was good-looking and extremely dainty, and said that she was rich; although she was really, as it turned out, none of these things, but was only so in semblance.'

Blinded by his passion, Menipus did not realise his impending fate, but his friend Apollonius, whose judgment was not be-clouded by sexual desire, warned him: '. . . This fine bride is one of the vampires, that is to say of those beings whom the many regard as *lamias* and hobgoblins. These beings fall in love, and they are devoted to the delights of Aphrodite, but especially to the flesh of human beings, and decoy with such delights those whom they mean to devour in their feasts.'

In the end she confessed to Apollonius that she was indeed a vampire, and made the source of the lore even more clear by stating that she was 'fattening Menipus up with pleasures before devouring his body, for it was her habit to feed upon young and beautiful bodies, because their blood is so pure and strong'.

Philostratus explains that he recorded the case in such detail because 'many people are aware of it and know that the incident occurred in the centre of Hellas; but they have only heard in a general and vague manner that he [Apollonius] once caught and overcame a lamia in Corinth'.

But it is *The Odyssey* that contains the clearest statement of the close link between the un-dead and the reputedly magical pro-perties of blood, and provides an explanation of why vampires were believed to subsist on it by the people of ancient Greece and Rome.

In the Limbo, which lies between Hades and the living world, Odysseus met the spirits of the dead. They had their erstwhile shape but not the energy to speak. It was blood alone that could lend them the vitality necessary for speech. Odysseus dug a pit and filled it with the blood of sacrificial sheep, which he had to guard with his sword against the throng of silent spirits until Tiresias had had his fill. The Theban also told him that a drink of the blood would confer upon the un-dead at least some of the faculties of the living.

Although the writers of antiquity do not seem very consistent in distinguishing between the various kinds of vampires, witches, ghosts and other praeternatural creatures haunting them, they were quite convinced that Lamiae sacrificed to Hecate, the goddess of death. In fact there was in Rome a college of clairvoyant priests especially skilled in combating Lamiae. The *Jus Pontificum* forbade Romans 'to leave the dead exposed to the claws of Strygae or Lamiae'.

The overlapping characteristics of these un-dead creatures include, apart from their propensity to temporary corporeal incorruption, most of the peculiar qualities attributed by Hungarian and Slavonic superstitions to their home-grown brand of vampires. The inconsistencies of the writers of antiquity can be observed, in a compounded form, in the virtually identical charges brought against vampires in the Dark Ages, witches and sorceresses in the Middle Ages, ogres, heretics and witches during the Renaissance, were-wolves in the sixteenth and seventeenth centuries and vampires in the eighteenth century.

The advent of Christianity strengthened the popular belief in Europe in un-dead creatures rising from their graves. The early Christian chroniclers recorded many instances of excommunicated persons leaving their graves because their souls could find no rest. This belief in the existence of apparitions returning from their grave was based on a mixture of Church doctrine on the role of Purgatory and ancient European pagan traditions.

The early Fathers naturally took into consideration the general beliefs and superstitions prevalent among those they sought to convert, and, as they were just as much influenced by such beliefs as their contemporaries, they unwittingly passed them on in the guise of Christian doctrine. Their preoccupation with 'demons'—un-dead spirits of evil influence, to be placated with sacrifices—is particularly relevant.

St Paul, for instance, must have considered the votive offerings and sacrifices made to these demons of considerable importance to have warned the Corinthians that 'what you are sacrificing is a sacrifice to the demons, not to God'. But he made no attempt to dispel the prevalent belief in the existence of these malevolent creatures.

The homilies attributed to St Clemens help to explain the reason, commonly accepted by the early Christians, for the attacks of vampire 'demons' upon human beings. 'As these are spirits', says the saint, 'who want to partake of food and drink and feel the desire to do so but cannot as they are spirits and have no organs, they turn to humans to make use of their organs. Once in possession of suitable organs, they can obtain whatever they want and take it through the mouth of possessed humans'. What they wanted most, he averred, was blood, thus maintaining the ancient Greek belief that it was human blood which gave them the power of speech.

Such notions fitted neatly into the teachings of the Christian Church. The mystical transubstantiation of Christ's blood, offering all who drank of it absolution from original sin and the promise of eternal life, reflected the widely held belief in the regenerative power of blood. This was at the very centre of Christian ritual, and to this day priests celebrating Mass drink the incorruptible blood of Jesus Christ in the form of wine to assimilate his divine nature.

Because this belief in the magic qualities of blood became inextricably interwoven with the religious and secular cultures of Christian Europe* and gave rise to new superstitions, the role of the Gospel and certain theological dogmas in the establishment of a new type of vampire tradition cannot be too strongly emphasised. The Gospel of St John for instance, teaches:

'Then Jesus said unto them, verily, verily, I say unto you, except ye eat the flesh of the Son of Man, and drink his blood, ye have no life in you. Whoso eateth my flesh and drinketh my blood hath eternal life; and I will raise him up at the Last Day.

* Blood lores and vampire traditions of other, non-European civilizations are beyond the scope of this book.

For my flesh is meat indeed, and my blood is drink indeed. He that eateth my flesh and drinketh my blood dwelleth in me, and I in him. As the living Father hath sent me, and I live by the Father: so he that eateth me, even he shall live by me.' (VI. 53–7).

Not surprisingly, perhaps, cases of vampirism reflecting the antithesis of these religious notions about the mystical properties of blood were recorded mainly in Christian countries.

In the Dark Ages the exhortation to drink Christ's transubstantiated blood and eat his flesh were taken rather more literally than the Church had intended. Charlemagne, appalled by the effects on the Saxons of mixed pagan and Christian beliefs involving the ritual eating of human flesh, passed strict laws to prevent his newly acquired subjects from putting to death anyone suspected of being a *strige*, or sorceress feeding on human flesh. Under his laws all those believing that 'men and women were *striges* (vampires) or sorcerers, who ate human beings', were to be condemned to death: 'so should be those who burn them, or give their flesh to eat or eat it themselves'.*

The belief that ravenous vampires devoured people and drank their blood was widespread in Europe in the Dark ages, and many suspected vampires were burnt or otherwise put to death. The Slavonic tribes occupying the territory of present-day Russia used bread baked with the blood of these alleged vampires as protection against blood-suckers.

The Anglo-Saxons' preoccupation with fiendish half-human monsters feeding on human flesh and sustained by blood which they drank straight from their victims' veins is the central theme of the eighth-century Old English heroic saga *Beowulf*. Although the poet was clearly a Christian, the background of pagan beliefs breaks through the newer ethos in the portrayal of Grendel as the embodiment of demonic, primordial forces. The pagan *Grettis Saga* also contains clear references to the Norsemen's fear of un-dead vampires believed to inhabit ancient funeral mounds.

* * *

* *Capitul Caroli Magni pro partibus Saxoniae;* I. 6.: 'Si quis a diabolo deceptus crediderit, sicundum morem paganorum, virum aliquem aut feminam strigem esse, & homines comedere, & propter hoc ipsum incenderit, vel carnem ejus ad comedendum dederit, vel ipsum comederit, capitis sententia puniatur.'

With the spread of Christianity to the whole of Northern Europe, supplanting the local pagan beliefs, tales of vampire attacks became more frequent in Scandinavia and the British Isles. As the practice of excommunication increased, so did the reports of un-dead men returning from their graves.

That vampirism was basically a superstitious attempt to make tangible the nature and meaning of excommunication can be gleaned from clerical accounts of the life of St Libentius, an eleventh-century archbishop of Bremen.*

According to these he excommunicated a gang of North Sea pirates around the year 1000. One of them was, after his death, buried in Norway. Seventy years later his body was found to be still intact and, the chronicle notes, it did not fall to ashes until it had received absolution from the Bishop of Alvareda.

The sources of mediaeval vampirism were extended further through sinister blood healing beliefs based on the cult of the Virgin Mary and a corrupt interpretation of the promise of salvation through the drinking of Christ's blood. Physicians prescribed the drinking of uncorrupted virgins' blood or its external application as a magic antidote to many incurable afflictions. Maidens were killed, with or without their families' consent, for the miraculous substance in their veins, and the vampire lore went from strength to strength.

But the increasing secularisation of European culture transformed the Christian belief in eternal life into a refusal either to accept the limitations of physical death or to await patiently the Day of Judgment. Death was no longer welcomed as the gateway to eternal life. By breaking free from the narrow confines of a theocentric outlook man was beginning to discover his potential. Instead of the mediaeval preoccupation with heaven and hell, Renaissance humanists were inspired by human potentiality; man was exalted, not death. The rediscovery of the human body, so long considered a mere casing for the soul, naturally riveted popular attention upon the un-dead vampires. For they were reputed to be living on blood and this was seen as evidence of the possibility of the survival of the body *without* the soul.

* *Saecula 6. Benedict.* Part I, p. 131.

The Catholic belief that apparitions and ghosts were the spirits of the departed, allowed to return from Purgatory for some specific reason, was widely held during the Renaissance. But after the advent of Protestantism, such leading reformers as Calvin, Lavater and Reginald Scot challenged the accepted Catholic doctrine of the state of the soul after death by denying the existence of Purgatory. Having thus denied the possibility that those returning from the grave were actually the spirits of the departed, they had to provide an alternative explanation for the superstitions and ghosts, and in general, they treated the problem of vampires and other apparitions returning from the grave as part of the wider issue of witchcraft.

Nevertheless, the vampire phenomenon was examined with great thoroughness by Protestant theologians, and a fresh attempt was made to define its nature. Hedged in by the precepts of the Reformation, these investigations got no closer to the truth than the Catholics had done in the preceding centuries. The desire to rid Christianity of old errors and primitive mediaeval dogmas resulted in the creation of new fallacies which were used to a great extent in justifying the horrors of witch-hunts in Protestant countries. James I of England* reflected in his writings the general tenor of Protestant views, according to which ghostly apparitions were devils who assumed the form of departed relations and friends in order to cause physical or spiritual harm to those whom they visited.

Louis Lavater, who wrote in the sixteenth century the most exhaustive study of vampire apparitions and other deadly spirits, noted the common pitfalls of earlier investigations, but remained firmly convinced of the existence of un-dead apparitions, thus assuring the survival of vampire superstitions.

'Many which neuer sawe or hard any of these thinges', he wrote,† 'suppose all that is reported of them, to be meere trifles and olde wyves' tales: for so muche as simple men, and suche as are fearful and superstitious, persuade themselues they haue seene this or that, when in deede the matter is otherwise. Againe,

* James the First: *Demonologie*, Edinburgh, 1597.
† L. Lavater: *Of ghostes and spirites walking by nyght*, English edition of 1572.

there are some which as soone as they heare of any thing, especially if it happens in the nyghte, they by and by thinke some spirite doth walke, and are maruellously troubled in mynde, because they can not discerne naturall things from spirites.

'And some (cheefly those which hunt after gaynes, by the soules of deade men) affirme that the most parte such thynges which are hard or seene, are soules of dead men, whych craue helpe of them that are liuing, to be deliuered out of the torments of most cruell payne in Purgatorie. Many not only of the common sorte, but also menne of excellent knowledge, do maruayle whether these bee any spirits or no, and what manner of thyngs they are.'

Lavater concluded that these apparitions preying on humans were definitely not the souls of dead men, but 'either good or euill Angels, or else some secrete and hid operations of God'.

Although his common sense led him to see that there were many earthly factors that caused men, and in particular priests, to disguise themselves as apparitions, his final conclusions were befogged by theological maxims. 'Many times, pleasant and merrie men', disguise theselues like Deuils, or else shroud theselues in white sheetes to make other men afrayde: with whome if simple men chance to meete, they make no doubt of the matter, but uerily thinke they haue seene spirites, and strange sightes. And yet it is not alwayes the safest way so to deceyue men with iests and toyes, for many examples myght be brought to shew how euill some men haue sped hereby. It is usual and common thing that young men merily disposed, when they trauell by the way, coming to thyr Inne at night, tye roapes to the bed side, or to the couerlet or garments, or else hide theselues under the bed, and so counterfeiting them selues to bee Spirites, deceyue and mocke their fellows. . . . Moreouer, it is well knowen to all men, that harlets, and whooremongers have practised their wickednesse a long season under this cloake and pretence.

'To these things may be added that ther have bene in al ages certain priests, which practising straunge deuises, & giuing themselues to Necromancie, have bewitched foolishe men that highlie esteemed them, to the ende they might thereby encrease their riches, and followe their lustful pleasures.

'To al the premisses before handled, this also is to be added, which no man cã deny, but ye many honest & credible persons of both kinds, aswel men as women, of whom som ar liuing & som already departed, which haue & do affirm that they haue some times in the day, & sometimes in the nyght seen & hard spirits. Some mã walketh alone in his house, & behold a spirit apeereth in his sight. . . . Some men goeth to bed, and laieth him down to rest, and by the by there is some thing pinching him, or pulling off clothes; sometimes it sitteth on him, or lyeth downe in the bed with him: and many times it walketh up and downe in Chamber. There haue bene many times men seen, walking on foote, or riding on horseback, being of a fierce shape, knowen unto divers men, & suche as died not long before.

'And hereby it may be proued, that they were not Priestes, or other bolde and wicked men, whiche haue fayned themselues to be soules of men deceased, as I haue before saide, in so muche that euen in those mennes chambers when they haue been shut there haue appeared such things, when they haue with a candle diligently searched before, whither any thing haue lurked in som corner or no. Many use to this day to serch and sifte, euery corner of the house before they go to bed, ye they may sleep more soundly: & yet neuerthelesse, they heare some scrying out, and making a lametable noise &c.'

The vampire ghost controversy was soon overshadowed by the great witch scare that spread across Protestant countries. But in other parts of Europe, both in the west and in the east, vampire attacks continued to be reported with astonishing regularity. Sixteenth-century French chroniclers, among them Daubigné and Sulli,* recounted frightening attacks by alleged apparitions returning from the grave in Rouen, Dijon and Navarre. Spain and Ireland, too, had their share of vampire troubles. In Ireland the fact that people who died unshriven and unbaptised children were not buried in consecrated ground had a great deal to do with the popular belief in the un-dead leaving their graves.

* Daubigné: *Histoire Universelle*, Paris, 1574.

Reports of the un-dead harrying the living were most frequent, however, in Eastern Europe. There, according to popular belief, the outbreak of vampirism could in most cases be traced to were-wolves. Lycanthropy, the ability of a human being to change into a wolf in order to gratify his craving for blood, was considered a commonplace occurrence in the Carpathians and the Balkan peninsula. Under the influence of the moon the lycanthropus would fall into a trance and his soul would enter that of a wolf in search for human blood. At cock-crow it would return to the body and revert to normal human shape. But after death the were-wolf became a fully-fledged vampire.

Lycanthropy was not a new phenomenon in Eastern Europe. Avicenna, one of the most outstanding of mediaeval philosophers and physicians, wrote of this affliction, which he called 'Cucubuth'. Men affected by it, he claimed, run howling about the graves at night and will not be persuaded that they are not wolves, and he noted that the malady was most frequent in Hungary and Bohemia, particularly in the month of February.

The sixteenth-century Serbs of the Balkan peninsula, unlike most other Europeans, did not differentiate between were-wolves and vampires, lumping both together under the generic term of *vlkoslak*, and the Czechs of Bohemia used the word *vilkodlak* to describe both. The Greeks, upon whom the vampire tradition had maintained its hold since classical times, used the Slavonic loan-word of *vrykolakas* both for the apparitions returning from the grave and for were-wolves, though the people of Crete retained their own word, *katakhanas*, for the blood-sucking vampires.

Sigismund, the Holy Roman Emperor and King of Hungary, who thought the stake the best remedy for the heresy of Reformation in the Czech Lands, saw to it that lycanthropy was included among the matters encompassed by Church dogma. He called a council of leading theologians to discuss the phenomenon and pronounce the Church's infallible ruling on were-wolves. After long deliberation the theologians decreed unanimously that anyone who denied that a human being could transform himself into a were-wolf was guilty of heresy. The standard punishment for heresy under Sigismund was burning at the stake.

Between 1520 and the middle of the seventeenth century some thirty thousand cases of lycanthropy are known to have been investigated by the Roman Church. Their trials hardly differed in scope or purpose from those of the witches in Western Europe.

Towards the end of the seventeenth century reports of dead men returning from the grave multiplied alarmingly. Chroniclers of the period clearly stated that these vampires were 'spectres of men that come again in the body'. They were suddenly sighted everywhere in Hungary, Bohemia, Poland and Silesia, maltreating humans and animals alike. The only other European country in which vampire attacks were on the increase was Greece, where sightings coincided with Church-inspired rumours that 'vampires were excommunicated persons whom the Earth is said to cast up'.

The French journal, *Mercure galant*, in its 1693–4 issue gave considerable coverage to the growing incidence of vampire attacks in Eastern Europe. 'The vampires' it declared, quoting from travellers' reports, 'appeared after lunch and stayed until midnight, sucking the blood of people and cattle in great abundance. They [the vampires] sucked through the mouth, the nose but mainly through the ears. They say that the vampires had a sort of hunger that made them chew even their shrouds in the grave.'

Erasmus Franciscus, in his appraisal of the work of the seventeenth-century Baron Valvasor,* described the case of a Carniolese peasant who, after his sudden death, plagued his friends and relations. The Church authorities eventually opened his grave, where his body was found intact although he had been buried for several months. When the public executioner cut off the alleged vampire's head his body jerked as if he had been alive.

Although were-wolves were initially blamed for the spread of vampirism in Central and Eastern Europe in the seventeenth century, the festering schism between the Roman and Greek Orthodox Churches unwittingly lent a new dogmatic support to this phenomenon and associated beliefs. The two Churches, brought into a head-on collision on the territories liberated from the Turks in 1686 by the allied Christian armies led by Prince

* Baron H. Valvasor: *Die Ehre des Herzogthums Krain*, Leibach, 1689,

Eugen von Savoya, were soon locked in battle for the souls of Christians who, during the Islamic occupation, had left the fold of the Roman Church. With both Churches claiming that those buried in the unhallowed ground of the other could not rest in peace, popular fear and interest in these un-dead vampires grew out of all proportion to their alleged occurrence.

Dom Augustin Calmet, the abbé of Senones in Lorraine, writing in the late 1740s on the East European vampire infestation, helped to pinpoint the actual date—and thereby the possible cause—of the first persistent reports. According to him* these began in Hungary, Moravia and Silesia some sixty years earlier, that is, at the very time when the confrontation between the Roman and Greek Orthodox Churches began to reach crisis proportions.

In devoutly Catholic Poland, too, the first reports of un-dead people returning from the grave came from the eastern territories taken from Orthodox Muscovy, which styled itself the 'Third Rome' and true repository of purified Christiantiy. In the occupied lands conquering Catholicism and crusading Ortho- doxy found themselves in enforced physical contact for the first time, and rumours of vampire attacks soon followed. Father Gabriel Rzaczynski, a learned Polish Jesuit, described several alleged blood-sucking incidents by *upiers*, or 'dead men who, while already in their graves, are lustful, and similar ghosts who kill living human beings'†. But the decisive victory of King Bátori over the Orthodox Tsar Ivan in the previous century had limited the contacts between the two Churches and precluded the development of a full-blown vampire epidemic.

Dom Calmet clearly recognised that the dogmatic argument whether excommunicants putrefied in their graves or not had quite a lot to do with the increasing numbers of undead people believed to have returned from the grave.

---

* Dom Augustin Calmet: *Dissertations sur les apparitions des anges, des démons & des ésprits. Et sur les revenants et vampires de Hongrie, de Bohème, de Moravie & de Silésie*, Paris, 1746.

† G. Rzaczynski: *Historia naturalis curiosa regni Poloniae, & magn. Ducat Lithuaniae annexarumque Provinciar*, Sandomir, 1721.

'It is asserted by the modern Greeks, in defence of their schism, and as a proof that the gift of miracles and the Episcopal Keys subsist in their church more visibly and evidently than in the Church of Rome, and that with them the bodies of excommunicated persons never rot, but swell up to an uncommon size, and are stretched like drums, nor ever corrupt or fall to dust till they have received absolution from some bishop or priest. And they produce many instances of carcasses which have afterwards putrefied, as soon as the excommunication was taken off.

'They do not deny that a body's not corrupting is sometimes a proof of sanctity, but in this case they expect it to send forth an agreeable smell, to be white and ruddy, and not black, stinking and swelled like a drum, as the bodies of excommunicated persons generally are.'*

The blood-sucking vampires, and in their wake the strange controversy about the state of excommunicated bodies, soon spread to Western Europe. Voltaire, in his *Dictionnaire Philosophique*, summed it all up thus:

'For a long time the Christians who practised the Greek ritual believed that the corpses of those Christians who practised the Latin ritual would not decompose when buried in Greece, because they were excommunicated. This is precisely the contrary of what we, the Christians of the Latin ritual, think. We believe that corpses that remain intact bear the mark of eternal felicity.'

The ordinary people, unable to follow the twists and turns of dogmatic religious arguments, believed naturally enough that a body that does not decompose is suspect, and acted accordingly. In the eighteenth century graves were opened with growing frequency and the host of people accused of being un-dead might give the impression that Europe was suddenly beset by these strange apparitions. The number of suspected un-dead was swelled by suicides, heathens, Jews, Freemasons, Moslems and a host of transgressors of social taboos and Church rules, further increasing popular interest in this seeming flaw in the scheme of things. By the late 1720s vampirism appeared to have spread like a pestilence across Hungary and the neighbouring states of the Hapsburg

* Dom A. Calmet: op. cit., English edition, 1759.

empire. The terror wrought by the attacks of these un-dead creatures, presumed not to be subject to the general laws of nature, was heightened by the speed with which this contagion was spreading.

A few well-attested cases, recounted in great detail by the Count of Cabreras, one of the Imperial officers who conducted vampire investigations, to a Freiburg University professor in Brisgau in 1730, contain all the features that characterised hundreds of similar incidents in Hungary. At the request of Dom Calmet, the professor wrote the following account of what the count had told him:

'It is now fifteen years since a soldier, who was quartered in the house of a Haidamack peasant, upon the frontiers of Hungary, saw as he was at table with his landlord, a stranger come in and sit down by them. The master of the house and the rest of the company were strangely terrified but the soldier knew not what to make of it. The next day the peasant died, and upon the soldier's inquiring into the meaning of it, he was told that it was his landlord's father, who had been dead and buried for over ten years, that came and sat down at the table and gave his son notice of his death.

'The soldier soon propagated the story through his regiment, and by this means it reached the officers, who commissioned the Count of Cabreras, a captain in Allendetti's Regiment of Foot, to make an exact inquiry into the facts. The count, attended by several officers, a chirurgeion [surgeon] and a notary, came to the house and took the depositions of all the family, who unanimously swore that the spectre was the landlord's father, and that all the soldier had said was strictly true. The same was also attested by all the inhabitants of the village.

'In consequence of this, the body of the spectre was dug up and found to be in the same state as if it had been just dead, the blood like that of a living person. The Count de Cabreras ordered its head to be cut off and the corpse to be buried again.

'He then proceeded to take depositions against other spectres of the same sort, and particularly against a man who had been dead over thirty years, and had made his appearance several times in his own house at meal time. At his first visit he had fastened upon the neck of his own brother and sucked his blood; at his second, he had treated one of his children in the same manner, and the third time, he fastened upon a servant of the family; and all three died instantly.

'Upon this evidence, the count gave orders that he should be dug up; and being found like the first, with his blood in fluid state as if he had been alive, a great nail was driven through his temples and he was buried again. The count ordered a third person, who had been dead for over sixteen years, to be burned; and he was found guilty of murdering two of his own children by sucking their blood.

'The Commissioner then made his report to the general officer, who sent a deputation to Emperor Charles VI's court for further instructions; and the Emperor dispatched an order for a court, consisting of officers, lawyers, physicians, chirurgeons and some men of the clothes [priests], to go and inquire into the cause of these extraordinary events upon the spot.'

Two years later, in 1732, the Dutch journal 'Gleaner' compiled a list of vampire epidemics in Hungary, Moravia and Turkish Servia (Serbia). It told its readers that all the cases were well documented, and suggested that those who doubted them should consult 'the vast tomes' compiled by German physicians on this phenomenon or study the findings of inquiries undertaken by German academies of science and universities. Indeed, the number of learned treatises published in Germany between 1728 and 1734 is staggering,* and is indicative of the wide European

---

* Karl Ferdinand Schertz's *Magia Posthuma*, printed in Olmütz in 1706, was the forerunner of a host of seventeenth-century studies of vampirism in Central Europe. It was followed by Michael Ranftius' *De masticatione mortuorum in tumulis liber*, Leipzig, 1728; John Christopher Rohlius' *Dissertatio de hominibus post mortem sanguisugis, uolgo dictis Uampyrea*, Leipzig, 1732; Johann Christian Stock's 1732 Jena edition of *Dissertatio de cadaueribus sanguisugis*, and two more German-language treatises published in Leipzig in 1732. In 1733 Johannes Heinrich Zopfius had his *Dissertatio de Uampyris Serviensibus* printed in Duisburg. Ranftius also published an enlarged version of his work in Leipzig in 1734, in German, under the title *Tractatus von dem Kauen und Schmatzen der Todten in Grabern, worin die wahre Beschassenheit der Hungarischen Vampyrs oder Blut-Sauger gezeiget.*

interest in the Hungarian vampire epidemic. In 1732 alone, at least six major works appeared in Leipzig, Jena and Nuremberg, minutely analysing the metaphysical and theological aspects of vampirism.

The authorities in Austro-Hungary, both ecclesiastic and secular, were baffled. It was considered, like all other epidemics which had in the past swept the country, to be a visitation sent upon the people by the Lord for their sins. As neither the causes nor the nature of pestilence, whether smallpox or cholera, were understood, penance and prayers were the usual remedies prescribed by the Hospitaller monks and village priests. At the outbreak of an epidemic, which usually followed in the wake of the foreign armies fighting in or crossing the country, groups of 'penitents' clad in shirts marked with a red cross were formed. They would go from village to village flagellating themselves and their fellow penitents and praying for the forgiveness of their sins. Other traditional remedies against epidemics, apart from the 'healing scourge', included treatment by vinegar, the chewing of bark, the erection of Holy Trinity columns (known as 'pestilence columns') and pilgrimage to the tombs of famous healing saints. These superstitious healing methods were commonly used in Hungary until the end of the eighteenth century.*

The ancient pagan ritual of lighting fires, known as 'living fire', and the burning of effigies of vampires, as a protection against outbreaks of plague and wasting diseases of cattle, were considered an infallible remedy by most Slavonic people. The lighting of 'living fires', known in parts of Germany and the British isles as 'need-fires', was denounced by the Church in the early Middle Ages as a heathen superstition, but the practice has lingered on.

In the ritual as practised in the lands of the South Slavs a vast bonfire of poplar and cornel wood was kindled, by a virgin maiden and a chaste boy of around 14. For the ritual to work and the fire to purify man and beast, the pair had to strip naked and

* Dr E. Schultheiss: 'The history of epidemics in Hungary', published in the Dutch scientific journal *Centaurus*, 1971.

start the fire by rubbing two pieces of wood together in a dark room.* When the bonfire had subsided, first the beasts were driven through it, then the villagers would use the cinders to blacken each other. The cinders were considered as a protecting purifying agent because the 'living fire' had burnt up and destroyed the harmful influences of the vampires and demons. But neither the 'living fire' nor the blackening ceremony were considered to have the power to actually destroy vampires.

Shortly before the outbreak of the Hungarian vampire epidemic, contagious diseases had taken an exceptionally heavy toll. Between 1692 and 1694 over thirty thousand of Prince Savoya's soldiers died in an outbreak of the Black Death. In 1708 smallpox and pestilence together claimed more than half a million victims, and a further epidemic of pestilence and smallpox in 1719 killed off half the population of Transylvania.

In the general fear and confusion, the authorities overlooked the fact that the vampire attacks were invariably reported from border areas where Catholic Hungarians and Orthodox Serbs and Walachs intermingled. The names of the alleged vampires were of Slavonic origin, indicating that they were followers of the Greek Orthodox rites. The fact that they came from villages which had lost their Hungarian population during the Turkish occupation and been colonised by Orthodox Slavs from Turkish Serbia did not strike the official investigators of vampire attacks as relevant. Yet it was common knowledge that these new communities were subject to considerable pressures from the Hungarian administration and the Catholic Hapsburg military who governed them after the Turks had been ousted from Central Europe. These pressures created a psychosis in which mysterious

* Sir James Frazer adduces proof that need-fires were kindled in the Scottish Highlands against cattle-disease even in the last century. In the island of Mull and in Caithness bonfires were kindled and sick heifers were sacrificed in a ritual believed to have provided a certain cure for the murrain. The need-fire was also considered the sole remedy for witchcraft. That both the custom of lighting protective fires and the performance of the ancient rituals still live on in Eastern Europe I observed at the camp-fires of the communist World Youth Festivals in the 1950s, when Slav youths would jump over the fires and walk ceremoniously around them. But the meaning of the tradition was already lost, for no one knew the reason for the fire-leaping.

Better Known Species of Vampires Believed to have Infested Europe in the Eighteenth Century

Name of species	Country	How it becomes a vampire	Approved method of disposal
Sampiro	Albania	Natural causes	Stake through heart
Nachtzehrer	Bavaria	Being born with a second skin	Coin in mouth, cutting off the head with axe
Ogoljen⎫ Mura ⎭	Bohemia		Burial at crossroads
Krvoijac⎫ Vepir ⎭	Bulgaria		Chain it to the grave with wild roses
Pijavica	Croatia	Incest with mother	Cutting off head and putting it between legs
Vilkodlak	Czech Lands		
Kuzlak	Dalmatia	Weaning before time	Transfixing with a hawthorn bough
Kathakano	Crete		Boiling head in vinegar
Brukulaco⎫ Vrykolako⎭	Greece		Cutting off and burning head
Lidérc nadály⎫ Vámpir ⎭	Hungary		Stake through heart; nail through temples
Vampiro	Italy		
Dearg-dul	Ireland		Piling stones on its grave
Vryolakas	Macedonia	Natural causes	Pouring boiling oil on it; driving nail in its navel

Name of species	Country	How it becomes a vampire	Approved method of disposal
Upier and Upierzyca	Poland	When born with teeth	Bury face downwards
Gierach (Stryz)	Prussia		Putting poppy seeds in grave
Myertovets Vurdalak Upierzhy	Russia	Son of were-wolf or witch Witchcraft	Transfixing it with a stake through chest Driving stake through heart; to be hit only once, otherwise revives
(a) Strigoiul b) Muronul	Rumania	Born out of wedlock to parents begotten out of wedlock	(a) Taking out its heart and cutting it in two; garlic in mouth, nail in head (b) Nail through forehead or stake through heart
Vukodlak	Slovenia		
Vlkoslak Mulo Dhampir	Serbia	Incest, or killed by were-wolf; being stillborn	Cutting off its toes; driving nail in its neck
Neuntoter	Saxony		Lemon in its mouth
Vampiro	Spain		No known remedy
Vampyr	Sweden		
Bruxsa	Portugal	Witchcraft	No known remedy

events became more acceptable than they would have been in a calm and rational atmosphere.

The epidemic, whatever its social and medical causes (see page 36), was real enough and took a heavy toll. People allegedly bitten by a vampire would fall into a death trance and die of galloping anaemia. Physicians had no real remedy to offer and quacks were doing a brisk business in talismans and anti-vampire ointments. Science, fettered by Church dogmas, could not explain the nature of the epidemic. Popular superstition, on the other hand, offered time-honoured remedies against vampirism. As a result, in the Age of Reason most people put their hopes into incantations and exorcising prayers.

TWO

Vampire Trials

Thirty years of religious wars shattered the fabric of seventeenth-century Central Europe. It needed time for the ravages of the terrible carnage to heal, and only the realisation by Catholics and Protestants alike that further attempts to spread the true religion by force of arms would in all probability destroy Christian civilisation gave the peace any permanence.

Hungary, whose central plains were still occupied by the Turks, was an exception and the crusade against Islam continued. After the routing of Kara Mustafa's grand army in 1683 and the liberation of Buda by the allied Christian armies, led by Prince Eugen of Savoy, in 1686, the Turks were finally driven out of Hungary. The devastation caused by a hundred and fifty years of Turkish rule, and the continued persecution of Protestants in the Hapsburg-controlled liberated territories contrasted sharply with the baroque splendour and peace enjoyed by Bavaria, Bohemia and Austria after the Thirty Years War.

The peace that gave a new chance to Central Europe and precipitated a sudden flowering of cultural activities did not extend to the south-east and east of the continent. Throughout the seventeenth century Poland carried the Roman Church's crusading torch against Muscovy, which was then aspiring to the spiritual leadership of Europe. Poland was also rent by a fratricidal war of succession at the beginning of the eighteenth century. The Christian nations of the Balkans, who followed the Orthodox Church, were to all intents and purposes quietly abandoned to the rule of the Sultan. After all, these people were schismatics in the eyes of the Catholic Hapsburgs, the only effective Christian power to confront Islam, and schismatics were considered both in Austria and in Hungary to be worse than infidels. The periodic campaigns and forays into Turkish-held Balkan countries were, after Prince Eugen's resounding victory at Belgrade, ill-conceived and half-hearted efforts. And Charles VI's desire to show goodwill to Russia involved the Hapsburg empire in a disastrous war with Turkey as a result of which strategically vital territories liberated by Prince Eugen in Serbia were once again ceded to the Sultan.

The Hapsburg war of succession at the beginning of the eighteenth century embroiled Central Europe in another round of bitter fighting. At once the fears for the very fabric of society were forgotten. The rulers, both temporal and spiritual, no longer felt inhibited about settling their religious and territorial differences by arms. The crusading princes of the Roman Church turned their attention to the festering dispute with the Orthodox rite Church. In the liberated territories of southern Hungary and Turkish Serbia, temporarily administered by the Catholic Hapsburg military commanders as part of Hungary, the Orthodox Church was in a very weak and disadvantageous position.

The vacuum left in southern Hungary after the driving out of the Turks was being filled by the Catholic Hapsburg administration in a rough and ready fashion. National and religious issues were exacerbated, the different ethnic and religious groups set against each other to suit Imperial interests. The main differences arose between the Catholic Hungarians, on the one hand, and on the other, the Orthodox South Slavs and Walachs, who replaced the Hungarian population in some of the devastated border areas. The antagonisms between the two churches, suddenly confronting each other within the boundaries of a nation-state, overrode the national differences between Hungarians and their Austrian overlords. Moreover, the Orthodox Church was tolerated under the Ottoman empire with its proselytising powers undiminished. To the Catholics, who fought in the vanguard of the allied Christian armies that liberated Hungary, they were not only schismatics but collaborators. The

protests of Orthodox-rite South Slavs against the blanket impo-
sition of Catholic tithes further aggravated the situation.

The Inquisition, the Roman Church's instrument for dealing
with schismatics and the like, was already in decline, the witch-
hunt in the Protestant territories was slowly abating and heresy
had lost much of the social dread attached to it. A vigorously
pursued and dogmatically justified campaign against the widely
feared vampires, however, offered a useful lever with which to
re-establish the Catholic Church's dominant position and reassert
its spiritual influence in the mixed border areas. With the motive
clearly established, there can be little doubt as to whom the
hunting down and prosecution of alleged un-dead vampires
benefited. The psychological weapon furnished by the nature of
the accusations was exploited to the maximum effect to belabour
the Orthodox rite Church. The trials also provided a legal forum
to discredit the fellow congregationalists of alleged vampires who,
in the recorded cases in Hungary's southern border areas, were
Slovenes, Serbs or other aliens.*

The trouble was that the widespread persecution of alleged
vampires created a general psychosis of fear which, in turn, was
instrumental in turning a popular superstitious belief into a real-
life epidemic with diagnosable symptoms. The contagion
eventually affected other territories in which the social composition and religious balances were different, and where its root
cause was no longer identifiable.

Initially, the local population took the law into its hands,
opened graves and destroyed the alleged vampires. Soon, however, a suitable legal frame was provided by the authorities.
Witnesses were summoned and depositions taken. Arguments
both for and against a person being an un-dead vampire were heard
and weighed against the collected evidence. Then the body would
be dug up and examined for the common marks of vampirism, believed to be a pliancy and flexibility of limbs, fluidity of blood and
unputrefied flesh. If these symptoms were positively identified,

* Petar Plogojowitz, a servant called Rhadek, a heyduck named Stanko, and
three women, Stanoska, Ruscha and Militsa, the accused of famous eighteenth-
century vampire trials, were all Slavs of Orthodox persuasion.

then the body would be delivered to the public executioner for burning or some other locally sanctioned form of destruction.

According to Karl Ferdinand Schertz* the vampire courts delayed the burying of suspected vampires, in some places for up to six or seven weeks. If at the end of that period it was found that their limbs were still supple and their blood liquid, they were then burnt on a stake.

The vampire courts were composed of Imperial Army officers and ecclesiastic and legal officials. But as the documents compiled by these courts indicate, the vampire judges were not only influenced by Church dogmas, but also by the prevalent crude popular superstitions.

The officials received their information of alleged vampire infestations from local sources, mainly from priests whose reports passed easily from ascertainable facts to mere suppositions. The Imperial officials sent to south-east Hungary and other outlying parts of the Hapsburg empire to investigate local reports of vampire attacks were further hindered in their enquiries by the fact that they were unable to speak Hungarian or the tongues of the cohabiting nationalities.

The Imperial commission, formed in 1732 on the orders of Emperor Charles (VI) to investigate the vampire attacks linked with the heyduck Arnold Paul of Medreyga, included a number of civil servants, ecclesiastics and high-ranking army officials, among them Prince Karl Alexander of Würtemberg. It, too, relied on the testimonies collected by the local church authorities, as its members had no knowledge either of the region or the language spoken there. The case of a girl called Stanoska, daughter of heyduck Jotuitzo, who was the subject of one of the most widely publicised vampire trials of the eighteenth century, was heard by a tribunal of similar composition.

But in order to put the un-dead vampires on trial they had first to be recognised as the causes of the contagion. The actual ferreting out of the dangerous un-dead was invariably the task of local people, led, as a rule, by their village priests. They employed means, sanctioned by popular tradition, and compared to which

* Karl Schertz: *Magia Posthuma*, Olmütz, 1706.

the mediaeval ordeal by fire or water was a highly sophisticated instrument of justice. A Walloon officer of the Imperial Army stationed in south-east Hungary in the early 1730s described a vampire hunt in a letter* to a relation:

'It is your wish that I should give you exact details as to what has been happening in Hungary with regard to certain apparitions, who so often molest and slay people in that part of the world. I am in a position to afford you this information, for I have been living for some years in those very districts, and I am naturally of an inquisitive disposition.

'I have heard in my lifetime a thousand relations of facts, or pretended facts, concerning spirits and witchcraft; but out of the whole number have credited scarce one. Indeed, one cannot be too circumspect in this matter, without danger of being imposed upon. Nevertheless, there are some facts . . .

'As for these Hungarian spectres, the thing generally happens in this manner: a man finds himself fallen into a languid state, loses his appetite, decreases visibly in bulk and, at eight or ten days' end, dies without a fever or any other symptom of illness save anaemia and loss of flesh and a dried, withered body.

'In Hungary they say that a vampire has attacked him and sucked his blood. Many of those who fall ill in this way declare that a white spectre is following them and sticks to them as close as their own shadow. When we were in our Kalocsa-Bács quarters, in the county of Temesvár,† two officers of the regiment in which I was a cornet died from this langour, and several more were attacked and would have perished had not a corporal of our regiment put an end to these maladies by resorting to the remedial ceremonies which are practised by local people. These are very unusual, and although they are considered an infallible cure I cannot remember even having seen these in any ritual.

* *Les Lettres Juives*, 1732. These letters (or possibly articles in epistolary form) contained the views of enlightened Christians who presented their remarks on the customs and events of a European nation through the medium of a foreigner in order to avoid the bias inherent in the attitudes of natives.

† This territory then formed part of south-eastern Hungary, now part of Rumania, where Orthodox Serbs, Catholic Hungarians and Danube Germans and Orthodox Rumanians live in mixed communities.

'They select a young lad who is innocent of girls, that is to say who had never performed the sexual act. He is placed upon a young stallion who has not yet mounted a mare, who has never stumbled and who must be pitch-black without a speck of white. The stud is ridden into the cemetery to and from among the graves, and the grave over which the horse refuses to pass in spite of blows liberally administered to him, is where the vampire lies.

'The tomb is opened and they find a sleek, fat corpse, as healthily coloured as though the man were quietly and happily sleeping in calm repose. With one single blow from a sharp spade they cut off the head, whereupon there gushes forth a *warm* stream of blood of rich red colour, filling the whole grave. It could easily be surmised that they had just decapitated a big brawny fellow of most sanguine habit and complexion.

'When this business is done, they refill the grave with earth and then the ravages of the disease immediately cease, whilst those suffering from this malady gradually recover their strength, just as convalescents recuperate after a long illness.

'This is exactly what occurred in the case of our young officers who had sickened. As the colonel of the regiment, the captain and the lieutenant were absent, I happened to be in command just then and I was mightily vexed to find that the corporal had arranged the affair without my knowledge.'

The young officer's description provides incontrovertible proof of the sheer superstitious nature of the search for alleged vampires at the height of the epidemic. Like most Imperial officers stationed in Hungary, he did not speak Hungarian or Serbian, and furthermore he admits in his letter that he was not actually present at the exhumation to provide a reliable eye-witness account.

In Transylvania, which contained a sizable Walachian population following the Orthodox rite Church, similar methods were employed to track down vampires in their graves, while suspected victims of vampire bites who themselves could, in due course, have passed on the 'sickness' were given a test of an overtly religious nature. They were made to kiss an amulet depicting St George fighting the dragon; were asked to put three finger-tips on a crucifix and were closely observed to see if the skin turned brown as if by burning; and at the end of the test they had to repeat three times aloud the Lord's Prayer without a shiver or a shake before they were declared free of the contagion.

The prosecution of vampires acquired an anti-Protestant nature in Bohemia where the Roman Church, identifying itself with the imperial interests of the house of Hapsburg, was bent on the destruction of the new generation of Hussites who combined for the first time heresy with ideas of Czech national awakening.

Acts of vampirism were linked with witchcraft and, just as in the preceding centuries, when witch-hunts and trials were rife, the clergy were the main promoters of the prosecution against persons charged with this alleged heretic affliction. The Cardinal Bishop of Olmütz, in his report on vampire trials in Bohemia* in the 1730s and 1740s, confirmed this trend. The members of the tribunals were all clergymen.

'The ministers of religion', the report said, 'received exact information, and having formed a judicial assembly, pronounced a final sentence on the so-called vampire. Under this, and in accordance with all due forms, it was ordered that the public executioner should go to the place where the vampire was, open the tomb and with a sword, and in sight of public spectators, should cut off the head and then open his chest with a halberd and transfix the vampire's heart with an iron stake, striking through the breast, and then close the tomb. In this way the vampire would cease to appear, while many others who had not yet been judged and executed were still appearing and producing calamitous results like the afore-mentioned.'

It is significant that there was not a single trial which concerned itself with finding out the truth about the causes of vampirism or the nature of the contagion. Reason and reliable evidence in conflict with the Catholic Church's notions on the nature of vampirism were excluded. The sentences were based on the Catholic Church's view that vampires, like witches, depended for their strength and supernatural powers on the Devil, and that, therefore, it was God's will to destroy them.

* Giuseppe Davanzati, Patriarch of Florence: *Dissertatione sopra i Vampiri*, published by Filippo Raimondi, Naples, 1744.

But with typical mediaeval casuistry it was urged that, in His infinite wisdom, God permitted the existence of vampires just as he permitted the existence of evil on earth and allowed the Devil to tempt human beings. This not only explained why vampires were believed to be endowed by the Devil with supernatural powers but also justified the Church's crusade against them.

Vampires, it was claimed, were lurking in every cemetery, and their proselytising powers could only be checked by the Catholic Church. Plainly with the number of excommunicants growing and the other Christian churches preaching heresies, only the Catholic Church could combat this new mortal menace and assure the salvation of believers.

It was not only the vampire judges and theologians who accepted unquestioningly the un-dead nature of vampires. Otherwise enlightened and rational eighteenth century thinkers who addressed themselves to the host of attendant problems related to this phenomenon likewise had failed to come to grips with the nature of vampirism.

Living in a theocentric society, they conducted their investigations along theological lines. They failed to divest themselves of the prevalent religious dogmas, accepted as a premise the un-dead nature of vampires and examined their alleged activities within the framework of the Devil's challenge to God's order on earth.

Man was universally considered the battle ground between good and evil, and vampirism was conceived of as a clear-cut victory for evil. In these circumstances a thorough scientific examination of the nature, scope, main springs and motivation of such savage attacks on human beings was inconceivable.

The problems that seemed to attract most eighteenth century enquirers were mainly metaphysical: were the creatures returning from their graves the spirits or the actual bodies of the un-dead? How and why did these ghostly spirits appear to the living and what forces endowed them with supernatural powers? Were vampires' bodies spectral and if so why did they suck the blood of the living?

The consensus of eighteenth century Catholic opinion on this subject appears to have been a slightly modified version of the views held by mediaeval theologians. These visitors from the grave were considered to be the souls of dead men and women who had not yet departed to their final destination. Somewhat incongruously, however, the Protestant view that the Devil gave them their horrific powers for his own reasons was also quietly adopted. Their alleged ability to leave their closed coffins, and pass through six feet of earth without disturbing it in search of human victims, was accepted as axiomatic. What these later writers queried was whether these spirits that gorged themselves on human blood were 'natural' or 'miraculous' apparitions.

Dom Calmet, one of the most learned of the eighteenth century investigators of vampirism, dispelled in his major work many of the then prevalent superstitions concerning the un-dead, and proved, even if in an indirect way, how untenable were the theological disputations about the divine or evil nature of these creatures.

'Supposing, indeed, there were any truth in the accounts of these appearances of vampires', he wrote, 'are they to be attributed to the powers of God, to the angels, to the souls of those who return in this way or to the Devil? If we adopt that prevalent last hypothesis it follows that the Devil can imbue these corpses with subtility and bestow upon them the power of passing through the earth without any disturbance to the ground, of gliding through the cracks and joints of doors, of slipping through a keyhole, of increasing and diminishing, of becoming rarified as air or water to penetrate the earth; in short, of enjoying the same properties as we believe will be possessed by the blessed after Resurrection, and which distinguished the human body of Our Lord after the first Easter Day, inasmuch as he appeared to those to whom he would show himself.

'Yet even if it be accepted that the Devil can re-animate dead bodies and give them movement for a certain time, can he also bestow these powers of increasing, diminishing, becoming rarified and also so subtle that they can penetrate the earth, doors, windows?

'We are not told that God allows him the exercise of such

powers, and it is hard to believe that a material body, gross and substantial, can be endowed with this subtlety and spirituality without some destruction or alteration of the general structure and without damage to the configuration of the body. But this would not be in accord with the intention of the Devil, for such change would prevent this body from appearing, from manifesting itself, from motion and speech, indeed, from being eventually hacked to pieces and burned as so often happens in the case of vampires in Moravia, Poland and Silezia.'

Although Dom Calmet dispelled the more irrational notions associated with the vampire phenomenon, he failed, perhaps because of his position in the Church, to break free from the religious dogmas fettering rational examination. He saw that the supposedly supernatural powers of vampires did not fit into the immanent laws by which the system of things was governed. All the same, he shrank from spelling out that both the un-dead and their supposedly supernatural powers existed nowhere but in the imagination of ignorant and superstitious men.

A careful and unbiased examination of all recorded eighteenth-century vampire investigations would reveal a marked lack of reliable first-hand evidence concerning actual attacks by un-dead creatures. The intact bodies disinterred on suspicion of vampirism were not, in my view, in some sort of mystical vampire condition, but belonged, more likely than not, to unfortunate people who had been buried alive. Reports of people declared to be dead who revive in the morgue are quite common even in our medically advanced times, and it is quite understandable that gravely-ill patients and people subject to epileptic and other fits were buried alive in remote villages in eighteenth-century eastern Europe.

If they were lucky they died soon, either because of their illness or as a result of asphyxiation due to the premature internment. Those in a kind of suspended animation on the border of life and death (catalepsy) could have stayed intact for a considerable time without particularly damaging effect on their bodies. On regaining consciousness, however, in some cases perhaps several days or even weeks after burial, they would naturally try to claw their way out of their tomb, and this would explain the fresh blood on their faces and their hands. The mass of evidence adduced by the vampire tribunals charged with opening the graves of suspected vampires confirms no more than this.* And the alleged un-dead vampires, freshly dug up from their graves, who, according to the vampire tribunal reports, jerked and cried out under the executioner's stake, were the sorry victims of burial alive who came to in the moment of their execution. Naturally, fresh blood would gush forth from their severed heads as if, to quote the Walloon officer's report, 'they had just decapitated a big brawny fellow of most sanguine habit and complexion'.

Coloman the Learned, an enlightened twelfth-century Hungarian monarch well ahead of contemporary European thinking, dispelled the witch-hunting epidemic of his time with a simple statement from the throne: 'There are no such things as witches.' A similarly straightforward statement, that there are no such things as un-dead vampires, should put paid to the myth of un-dead creatures returning from their graves to suck the blood of the living. For an explanation of the vampire phenomenon, however, one has to look to the living.

Given the superstitious beliefs of eighteenth century Austria–Hungary and the suggestive nature of the affliction, a trained psychologist would justifiably look—apart from religion itself—to the psychosis of fear in general and the psychosis of mass hysteria in particular for a rational explanation.

Dr Herbert Mayo, senior surgeon at the Middlesex Hospital in the middle of the last century, examined the link between superstitious auto-suggestion and the reported physical symptoms of alleged vampire victims, in order to clear up the physical aspects of this malady. The death-like trance into which those allegedly bitten by a vampire during the great vampire epidemic used to fall, and even the galloping anaemia—although he does not go quite so far—have a joint psychological explanation.

* They paid, however, a great deal of attention to the chemical composition of the soil in order to rule out the possibility of natural causes in the preservation of the dead bodies. A list of the number of decayed bodies belonging to people who were buried around the same time in the same churchyard as the alleged vampire was usually appended to the reports.

'There is no reason', he wrote,* 'why death-trance should not, in certain seasons and places, be epidemic. Then the persons most liable to it would be those of weak and irritable nervous systems. Again a first effect of the epidemic might be further to shake the nerves of weaker subjects. These are exactly the persons who are likely to be infected with imaginery terrors, and to dream, or even to fancy, they have seen Mr or Mrs such a one, the last victim of the epidemic.

'The dream or impression upon the senses might again recur, and the sickening patients have already talked about it to their neighbours before they themselves were seized with a death-trance. On this supposition the Vampyr visit would sink into the subordinate rank of a mere premonitory symptom.'

With the death-trance divested of its mysterious nature and the alleged vampire visit reduced to an imaginary terror reflecting the most talked-of topic of the time, the loss of appetite and galloping anaemia could be explained on purely medical grounds without recourse to the mystique of a contagion spread by the bite of un-dead creatures.

There remains, however, one solid and incontestable fact which was observed in virtually all properly recorded cases. The attack on the afflicted person by a 'known vampire' usually, but not exclusively, began with kisses on the victim's throat. The kisses would eventually turn into a bite, and the gushing blood would be sucked by the vampire. There were never any complaints of pain recorded. On the contrary, most reports spoke of a kind of euphoric delirium into which the victim would slip during the blood-sucking act.

Cleansed of its superstitious and mystical trappings and placed in the context of sexual fantasy into which it undoubtedly belongs, the kiss-turned-bite provides the only reliable indication regarding the true nature of vampirism. The link between blood and sexual excitement, love-bites and kiss was well known in the eighteenth century.

The Marquis de Sade, in his *Justine, ou les Malheurs de la Vertu*,

* Dr Herbert Mayo: *On The Truth Contained in Popular Superstitions*, London, 1851.

and also in *Juliette*, used the vampire theme with a clear sexual undertone. In *Justine*, for example, de Sade's protagonist, the Comte de Gernade, takes an obvious sexual pleasure in watching the blood flow from the veins of his victims. The Marquis himself, after whom the lust to hurt and the sexual joy in the sight of the partner's blood has been named, could only make love to his women if he could prick them or cut them with a sharp object until blood spurted.

The relationship between kiss and bite is—as was recognised by Freud—the most fundamental in the whole range of sexual psychology. Psychologists maintain that the linking of these two instinctive acts is consistent with normal life. But the love-bite, again a perfectly healthy sexual manifestation, can easily slip into the region of the morbid and pathological, to trigger off a host of perverse impulses of which vampirism is one.

No one made the link between the kiss and the vampire bite more immediate and palpably real than Heinrich von Kleist, an eighteenth-century Prussian officer and dramatist. His *Penthesilea* provides a masterful portrayal of the awakening of the vampire instinct in a beautiful young woman during a moment of rare passion. Penthesilea, the Amazon queen, is in love with young Achilles, and mistakenly thinks he has rejected her. In her confusion she challenges to single combat, 'with all the terrors of weaponry', the youth whom she really wanted to make love to and cherish more than anything else.

> Den Zahn schlägt sie in seine weisse Brust,
> Sie und die Hunde, die wetteifernden,
> Oxus und Sphynx den Zahn in seine rechte,
> In seine linke sie; als ich erschien,
> Troff Blut von Mund und Händen ihr herab.

Having set the dogs on Achilles, she 'strikes her teeth into his white breast; she and her dogs—they on the right, she on the left; and . . . blood dripped from her mouth and hands.' Penthesilea's inadvertent passing from the intended love kiss to an act of savage vampirism indicates the thin dividing line between the two impulses: 'Did I kiss him to death' she asks, after having been

swept off her feet by a terrifying impulse. 'Did I not kiss him?
Or did I tear him to pieces? If so it was a mistake; for kissing
rhymes with biting, and whoever loves with her whole heart
might mistake the one for the other.'

> Mit diesen kleinen Händen hätt'ich ihn-?
> Und dieser Mund hier, den die Liebe schwellt-?
> Ach, zu andern Dienst gemacht, als ihn -! . .
> Küsst' ich ihn tot?
> Nicht? Küsst' ich nicht? Zerrissen wirklich? Spricht!
> So war es ein Versehen. Küsse, Bisse,
> Das reimt sich, und wer recht von Herzen liebt,
> Kann schon das eine für das andre greifen.

THREE

The Vampire in England and Scotland

Within a few years of the outbreak of the great vampire epidemic the general fascination with the nightmare existence of vampires was duly reflected both in fictional literature and in the then fashionable travelogues. The apparitions of ghosts and vampires, which greatly preoccupied the men of letters of central Europe, soon found their reflection in the works of German writers too. It proved a rewarding theme which attracted an avid readership.

One of the first to use the vampire motif successfully was Heinrich August Ossendorfer, a minor poet. In his poem 'Der Vampir'* he significantly described this strange affliction as originating in Hungary. The vampire hero of the poem even warned his maiden victim to 'believe in the deadly vampires as the people living along the river Tisza† do', and drank to their future vampire union in Hungarian Tokay wine.

Although the reference to the ecstatic vampire kiss—

. . . Alsdann wirst do erschrecken
Wenn ich dich werde küssen
Und als ein Vampir küssen

was carefully presented within a heterosexual love relationship, references to the girl's Christian beliefs and the vampire lover's opposed philosophies implied that the worlds they represented were in deadly competition. It was hinted that the death-like slumber into which the girl would fall after the first vampire kiss was not the end but the beginning of her real existence and that hint

* *Der Naturforscher, 48-es Stück*, Leipzig, 1748.
† The Tisza is one of Hungary's two major rivers.

expressed what many educated people of the time believed—that vampirism was a manifestation of a different kind of existence beyond the narrow limitations of the Christian interpretation of life and death, an existence parallel to that of the actual world.

Goethe was also greatly interested both in the physical and metaphysical aspects of vampirism. His ballad, 'Die Braut von Korinth' ('The Bride of Corinth'), successfully blended the classical vampire story of Phlegon of Tralles with the contemporary belief in the un-dead. Goethe's story had an unexpected side-effect in that it lent the theme, hitherto restricted to the oral tradition of peasant folk lore and minor poets, the stamp of the literary establishment. Vampire literature became respectable.

The vampire tradition, so widespread throughout the Continent, had no real roots in England. *Beowulf*, the eighth-century Old English heroic epic, provides, however, firm evidence that the Germanic tribes from which the Anglo-Saxons descended had brought with them from the Continent a superstitious fear of mythical dragons and evil, half-human monsters, feeding on human flesh and addicted to drinking human blood.

As the conversion of the Anglo-Saxons to Christianity must have been a comparatively recent event at the time of the writing of the poem, *Beowulf* is a repository of pagan Anglo-Saxon beliefs, with the newly imposed Christian teachings still barely expressed. The central theme of the poem is Beowulf's fight against Grendel, the fiendish half-human creature, revealing the Anglo-Saxon's preoccupation with monsters.

Grendel, also referred to sometimes as a cruel demon, had 'horrible firelit eyes', superhuman strength and talons instead of hands. He was savage, exasperated and grim, according to the poet, and attacked humans in their sleep:

'The demon, a black shadow of death, prowled, lay in ambush, and plotted against young and old. Night after night he patrolled the fog-bound moors ... This malign outcast, like the enemy of man that he was, made frequent attacks and produced unspeakable havoc.'*

The description of Grendel's depredations is graphic and offers a

* *Beowulf*, a prose translation by David Wright, Penguin, 1957.

welcome pointer to the nature of the superhuman ogres and monsters so dreaded by the Anglo-Saxons. During one of his attacks on the King's hall the fiend snatched up a sleeping man, 'tore him apart in an instant, crunched the body, drank blood from his veins, and gulped it down in great bites until he had wholly swallowed the dead man, even the hands and feet.' After quenching his blood lust he 'slunk off to his hiding place to rejoin the fellowship of devils'.

The people were defenceless against the monster's rule of terror, and in their superstitious fear they 'promised sacrifices to the heathen shrines, praying to the Devil for help against the oppression which afflicted them all. Such was their practice—and such the hope of a heathen people. Hell was in their hearts; they knew nothing of a Creator, the true God, judge of all acts; nor did they know how to worship the glorious king of heaven. Woe to him whose perversity shall thrust his soul into the abyss of fire, with no hope of change or of consolation'. The anonymous poet of *Beowulf* was clearly a Christian.

The similarity between the Anglo-Saxons' sacrifices to the demons and devil-worshipping and the sacrifices against which St Paul had warned the Corinthians is too great to be accidental, and it underlines the common European origins of both.

Because of his own Christian beliefs and the social pressures to discredit the old heathen ways, the *Beowulf* poet inserted a didactic explanation of the origins of monsters at the very beginning of his poem. Grendel, he preached, was an unhappy being who had long lived in the land of monsters 'because God had damned him along with the children of Cain. For the eternal Lord avenged the killing of Abel. He took no delight in that feud, but banished Cain from humanity because of his crime. From Cain were hatched all evil progenies: ogres, hobgoblins and monsters.' This fiendish monster attacked humans because their happiness and their song of Creation praising the Lord 'grated on his ear'.

It was a neat explanation with a moral message that should have gone down well with the Christian upper crust of Anglo-Saxon society to whom the poet would have recited his poetry at banquets and other festive occasions. But the bard was not consistent in maintaining a Christian explanation of the blood-drinking ogre's real nature.

Grendel's mutilated body, laid out by his mother after his defeat by Beowulf, showed the vital traits of *un-dead* Continental vampires. Instead of holy water, the poet resorted to the known heathen remedy—decapitation—to make him give up his ghost: 'The corpse bounded up at the sword stroke, and Beowulf severed its head as it lay lifeless. Another pointer to the heathen Anglo-Saxon notions about Grendel's true nature is that the poet calls his mother a 'she-wolf', linking her, however casually, with lycanthropy. The surviving English folklore is however, singularly devoid of were-wolves—the forerunners of vampirism in Germanic and east European popular belief. Notions of lycanthropy appear to have been reintroduced into the country by the waves of invading Norsemen whose Scandinavian sagas contain many were-wolves and blood-sucking apparitions. Sabin Baring-Gould* attributed the lack of were-wolf stories to the destruction of wolves by Saxon and early mediaeval English kings throughout England. Once extirpated, wolves ceased to exercise peoples' imagination, and their objects of dread were not endowed with the wolf's ferocity and blood-thirstiness.

Cases of vampirism were more generally noted after the Norman conquest. But all the references to acts of vampirism in twelfth-century English chronicles reflect the common Continental beliefs shared by Bretons, Hungarians, Slavs and Germans, indicating that vampirism was an imported tradition. Even the belief that vampire attacks, owing to the foetid state of the returning bodies, bring in their wake the pestilence, was present in all Continental traditions.†

* Sabin Baring-Gould: *Book of Were-Wolves*, London, 1865.
† The mediaeval belief that un-dead apparitions from the grave were harbingers or carriers of pestilence was still prevalent in central Europe in the sixteenth century. Lavater described the origins of one spate of rumours that swept his home town of Trigurine, in the district of Berne, in the 1560s. 'It chanced once', he wrote, 'that certayne pleseaunt young men disguising themselves, danced aboute the Churchyarde, one of them playing on a beere with two bones, as it were on a drume. Which thing when certaine men espied, they noysed it about the citie, how they had seene dead men daunce, and that there was greate daunger, least there should shortly ensue some plague or pestilence.'

William of Newburgh's contemporary account of twelfth-century *sanguisugae* (blood-suckers) haunting the people of England provides enough proof to assume that the fear of the effects of excommunication had just as much to do with the spread of the belief in vampires as the general cultural effect of the invading Normans. In his chronicle Newburgh recorded with the thoroughness of the tradition established by the Venerable Bede cases which he had heard from trusted and reliable priests, who had first-hand knowledge of the events. Nonetheless, these were not eye-witness accounts.

In the year 1196, during the reign of Richard I, Newburgh wrote of 'the extraordinary happening when a dead man wandered abroad out of his grave'* in Buckinghamshire. The incident was related to him by Stephen, the archdeacon of the diocese. William writes:

'A certain man having died, according to the course of nature, was by the seemly care of his wife and relations decently buried on the Eve of Ascension Day. But on the following night he suddenly entered the room where his wife lay asleep and, having awakened her, he not only filled her with the greatest alarm but almost killed her by leaping upon her with the whole of his weight and overlying her. On the second night also he tormented the woman in just the same way. Wherefore in the extremity of dread she resolved that on the third night she would remain awake and that then and thenceforth she would protect herself from his horrible attack by providing a company of persons to watch with her. Nevertheless, he visited her; but when he was driven away by the shouts and cries of those who were keeping watch, so that he could do her no harm, he swiftly departed. Having been thus baffled and repulsed by his wife, he proceeded in exactly the same manner to harrass and annoy his brothers who resided in the same town.'

The brothers defended themselves from the vampire's visits by sitting up all night and making a noise. As a result he appeared to several townspeople in broad daylight. The archdeacon wrote a

* *Historia Rerum Anglicarum*, Book V.

letter to the Bishop of Lincoln requesting his direction in combating 'so intolerable an evil'.

'When the Bishop heard of this he was greatly amazed, and
forthwith consulted with a number of learned priests and reverend
theologians, from certain of whom he learned that similar occur-
rences had often taken place in England, and many well-known
instances were quoted to him. They all agreed that the neighbourhood would never obtain any peace until the body of this miserable wretch had been disinterred and burned to ashes. However,
such a method seemed extremely undesirable and unbecoming
to the holy Bishop, who forthwith wrote out with his own hand
an absolution and sent this to the archdeacon, ordering that,
whatever might be the reason why this man wandered from the
grave, the tomb should be opened, and when the absolution had
been laid on the breast of the corpse, all should be fastened up as
before.

'Therefore they opened the tomb, and the body was found
therein uncorrupt, just as it had been laid upon the day of his
burial. The episcopal absolution was placed upon his breast, and
after the grave had again been fast closed, the dead man never
wandered abroad, nor had he the power to injure or frighten
anybody from that very hour.'

The similarity between Newburgh's vampire story and scores
of similar accounts in France, Spain and even in Norway (see
page 10) in the Middle Ages is too great to be coincidental. They
all involve excommunicated men unable to rest in their grave
until they receive absolution for their sins, and it seems reasonable
to assume that vampirism became something of a concern in
England for the first time under the new theocratic order established by the Normans.

Other transgressions of Church rules, and of social taboos, too,
are well represented among the vampire cases recorded by
Newburgh. They include a priest from Melrose Abbey who 'used
to hunt with horse and hounds' as if he were a layman; a most
infamous villain of Berwick-on-Tweed, who, because of his
unfair deals 'was indeed surpassing rich in this world's goods';
and the squire of Alnwick Castle. They were all sinners unable to

rest in their graves, and although they tormented the living and caused pestilence, their blood-sucking nature was only indicated by the constant epithet of *sanguisugae* used by Newburgh to describe them.

The squire of Alnwick Castle, whom Newburgh described as 'a stranger to God's grace and whose crimes were many', was given his unnatural powers by Satan.

'In the dark hours he was wont to come forth from his tomb and to wander about all the streets, prowling around the houses, whilst on every side the dogs were howling and yelping the whole night long. . . . The air became foul and tainted as this foetid and corrupting body wondered abroad, so that a terrible plague broke out and there was hardly a house which did not mourn its dead, and presently the town, which a little while before had been thickly populated, seemed to be well-nigh deserted, for those who had survived the pestilence and these hideous attacks hastily removed themselves to other districts lest they also should perish.'

The local priest, from whom Newburgh learned the story, called a council of devout men to find a means to rid the place of the vampire. While they were deliberating, the impatient young men of the town decided to exhume and burn him.

'They armed themselves, therefore, with sharp spades and betaking themselves to the cemetery, they began to dig. And whilst they yet thought they would have to dig much deeper, suddenly they came upon the body covered with but a thin layer of earth.

'It was gorged and swollen with frightful corpulence, and its face was florrid and chubby, with huge red puffed cheeks, and the shroud in which he had been wrapped was all soiled and torn. But the young men, who were mad with grief and anger, were not in any way frightened. They at once dealt the corpse a sharp blow with the keen edge of the spade, and immediately there gushed forth such a stream of warm red gore that they realised this sanguisuga had battened in the blood of many poor folk. Accordingly, they dragged it outside the town, and here they built a large pyre. . . . Now no sooner had that infernal monster been thus destroyed than the plague, which had so sorely ravaged the people, entirely ceased, just as if the polluted air was cleansed by the fire which burned up the hellish brute who had infected the whole atmosphere.'*

Between the twelfth and sixteenth centuries a few more Continental-style vampire stories were recorded in England, and Sir Thomas Malory revived the theme in a literary form in his *Morte d'Arthur*. The Vampire Lady encountered by Sir Lancelot and Sir Galahad during their peregrinations was clearly French, however, and there was nothing to link her, or her belief in the blood healing tradition, with England.

Over a century later, George Buchanan, Scotland's greatest humanist and James I's tutor, unmasked a rogue Scottish priest called Lang, who used the vampire threat to keep his congregation's mind on the torments of Hell. The priest travelled the length and breadth of the country, telling the people that 'in a field in Scotland full of Brimstone there are soules miserablie tormented, which continually crie for helpe and succor.' But the truth was, Buchanan wrote,† that the priest had suborned a peasant whom he presented at learned gatherings as one of the tormented souls returning to earth at night. The peasant, however, gave the game away while drunk and unable to guard his tongue. Buchanan's lampooning of the deceitful ways of the Catholic priest followed the trend set by Protestant theologians, debunking Catholic notions on the state of the spirit after death. The tale was written abroad after Buchanan had embraced Protestantism.

With no indigenous tradition to speak of, and without the rival dogmas of Eastern rite and Catholic churches to confuse the people about the fate of the dead buried in unhallowed ground, vampirism remained an imported literary tradition. In any case, the witch-hunt begun by James I in England soon eclipsed popular interest in the un-dead. Consequently the great vampire epidemic that swept across central Europe never caught on in Britain.

Stories of vampire attacks in Austria–Hungary began reaching

* Newburgh: op. cit.
† G. Buchanan: *The Franciscan Friar*, translated from the Latin by George Provand, Glasgow, 1809.

England in the middle of the eighteenth century. The *Travels of Three Englishmen*★ created quite a sensation and awakened general interest in these unfamiliar un-dead apparitions. The travelogue explained that 'Vampyres are supposed to be the bodies of deceased Persons, animated by evil Spirits, which come out of the Graves, in the Night-time, suck the Blood of many of the Living, and thereby destroy them. Such a notion', the travelogue cautiously hinted, 'will probably be looked upon as fabulous and exploded by many people in England.'

To convince British public opinion of the deadly threat posed by un-dead vampires, and to strengthen their own credibility, they begged leave to quote at length from a learned dissertation on the subject by Dr Zopfius, one of the foremost eighteenth-century authorities on vampirism:

'The Vampyres, which come out of Graves in the Night-time, rush upon People sleeping in their Beds, suck out all their Blood, and destroy them', the learned Essen headmaster† was quoted as saying in his 'extremely learned and curious dissertation.' 'They attack Men, Women, and Children, sparing neither Age nor Sex. The People attacked by them complain of Suffocation, and a great Interception of Spirit; after which, they soon expire. Some of them, being asked, at the Point of Death, what is the matter with them, say they suffer in the Manner just related from People lately dead, or rather Spectres of those People upon which, their Bodies, from the Description given of them, by the sick Person, being dug out of Graves, appear in all Parts, as Nostrils, Cheeks, Breast, Mouth, &c. turgid and full of Blood.

'Their Countenances are fresh and ruddy; and their Nails, as well as Hair, very much grown. And, though they have been much longer dead than many other Bodies, which were perfectly putrefied, not the least Mark of Corruption is visible upon them. Those who are destroyed by them, after their Death, become Vampyres; so that, to prevent so spreading an Evil, it is found requisite to drive a Stake through the Dead Body, from whence, on this Occasion, the Blood flows as if the Person was alive.

★ *Harleian Miscellany*, London, 1745.

† J. H. Zopfius: *Dissertatio de Uampyris Serviensibus*, Duisburg, 1733.

Sometimes the Body is dug out of the Grave and burnt to Ashes; upon which, all Disturbances cease.'

The fears of the travelogue's authors that their report would be looked upon as fabulous by the level-headed British public proved to be unfounded. The travelogue caused quite a sensation, and reports of vampires began mushrooming in newspapers and periodicals. The public loved it and the accounts of strange goings-on in cemeteries and ancient castles were taken at face value.

Secure in the knowledge that such visitations by un-dead creatures can occur only in wild and distant countries, British men of letters did not consider it necessary to investigate or challenge the vampire phenomenon. In fact the English Romantic Revival showed an extra-ordinary interest in these grotesque tales of horror. Inspired by a combination of the then fashionable German and French horror stories, Gothic gloom and tales of the supernatural, the vampire tradition came into its own in Britain.

English writers in search of the grotesque and uncanny turned for inspiration to Gothic castles peopled by men and women subjected to frightening visions of horror. Horace Walpole's *The Castle of Otranto* (1764) and Mrs Ann Radcliffe's *The Mysteries of Udolpho* (1794) paved the way for the romantic horror fiction which culminated in Bram Stoker's *Dracula*.

However, the first fictional vampire story to introduce the ghouls and bloodsuckers of Continental folk lore tradition into the fashionable literary world of early nineteenth century England was John-William Polidori's *The Vampire*. It was a contribution to a romantic ghost story competition between the Shelleys, Lord Byron and Dr Polidori himself, who was the latter's friend and physician. Mary Shelley, in her entry, *Frankenstein*, created a monster which has not been rivalled by anything written since by the practitioners of horror and science fiction.

Polidori's vampire, Lord Ruthwen, is a parody of Lord Byron's inclination to torment those whom he loved—a traditional trait, also, of vampires. The story, which appeared in 1819 and was published under Byron's name, leading to endless literary disputes regarding its authorship, contains all the mistaken beliefs that even people of learning and literary tastes shared about the un-dead.

In order to understand the grip of the vampire tradition on Victorian England, it is worth looking at the interpretation Dr Polidori put on the meaning and sources of this strange affliction in his introduction to the story:

'The superstition upon which this tale is founded is very general in the East . . . It did not, however, extend itself to the Greeks until after the establishment of Christianity [sic] and it has only assumed its present form since the division of the Latin and Greek churches; at which time, the idea becoming prevalent that a Latin body could not corrupt if buried in their territory, it gradually increased, and formed the subject of many wonderful stories, still extant, of the dead rising from their graves, and feeding upon the blood of the young and beautiful.

'In the West it spread, with some slight variation, all over Hungary, Poland, Austria and Lorraine, where the belief existed that vampyres nightly imbibed a certain portion of the blood of their victims, who became emaciated, lost strength, and speedily died of consumptions; whilst these human blood suckers fattened —and their veins became distended to such a state of repletion, as to cause the blood to flow from all passages of their bodies, and even from the very pores of their skins.

'In the London Journal, of March, 1732, is a curious, and, of course, *credible* account of a particular case of vampyrism, which is stated to have occurred at Madreyga, in Hungary. It appears, that upon an examination of the commander-in-chief and magistrates of the place, they positively and unanimously affirmed, that, about five years before, a certain Heyduke named Arnold Paul, had been heard to say, that, at Cassovia [Kosice, in Czechoslovakia] on the frontiers of the Turkish Servia [sic], he had been tormented by a vampyre, but had found a way to rid himself of the evil, by eating some of the earth out of the vampyre's grave, and rubbing himself with his blood.

'This precaution, however, did not prevent him from becoming a vampyre himself. . . . For, about twenty or thirty days after his death and burial, many persons complained of having been tormented by him, and a deposition was made, that four persons had been deprived of life by his attacks.

'To prevent further mischief, the inhabitants, having consulted their Hadnagi [Lieutenant], took up the body, and found it (as is supposed to be usual in cases of vampyrism) fresh, and entirely free from corruption, and emitting at the mouth, nose, and ears, pure and florid blood. Proof having been thus obtained, they resorted to the accustomed remedy. A stake was driven entirely through the heart and body of Arnold Paul, at which he is reported to have cried out as dreadfully as if he had been alive. This done, they cut off his head, burned his body, and threw the ashes into his grave.

'The same measures were adopted with the corpses of those persons who had previously died from vampyrism, lest they should, in their turn, become agents upon others who survived them.

'This monstrous rodomontade is here related, because it seems better adapted to illustrate the subject of the present observations than any other instance which could be adduced. In many parts of Greece it is considered as a sort of punishment after death, for some heinous crime committed whilst in existence, that the deceased is not only doomed to vampyrise, but compelled to confine his infernal visitations solely to those beings he loved most while upon earth—those to whom he was bound by ties of kindred and affection.'

The Byronesque Lord Ruthwen, Polidori's un-dead hero who comes back from his grave to claim his bride, was the first vampire to instil a feeling of thrilling horror in Victorian readers. The next was Keat's 'Lamia'. The writers of penny dreadfuls, mingling distorted facts and fancy, came into their own in depicting vampire horrors. Thomas Preskett Prest in *Sweeney Todd, the Demon Barber of Fleet Street* and *Varney the Vampyre, or The Feast of Blood* piled blood-curdling horror upon blood-curdling horror in the best hack-writer tradition—and the readers loved it.

Le Fanu's *Carmilla*, the first woman vampire story, published in Dublin in 1872, was the next step in the literary exploitation of this widespread superstition, and it eventually reached its peak in Bram Stoker's vampire *Dracula*.

PART TWO

FOUR

A Horror Writer's Stroke of Genius

Bram Stoker, actor, journalist, wit, author and man-about-town in Victorian London, had tried his hand at horror stories before mixing historical fact and penny-dreadful fiction in *Dracula*. Published in 1897, it was not only an instant success, but was recognised by fans and critics alike as a horror writer's stroke of genius. The Transylvanian ghoul became the ultimate in sophisticated Victorian horror fiction.

Modern man's preoccupation with the supernatural cannot alone account for *Dracula's* undiminished appeal to readers living in the technologically and scientifically advanced society of today. Nor can the ingredients of this macabre tale—fascination with blood and human vampires, unadulterated horror with clear sexual undertones and the quaint setting of the drama—explain it. It is Stoker's ability to create a sense of the possibility of the impossible and transcend man's mortal limitations that grip the reader. The genesis of the *vampire Dracula* theme offers a clue to its understanding.

As Mary Shelley wrote in the foreword of *Frankenstein*: 'Everything must have a beginning, to speak in Sanchean phrase, and that beginning must be linked to something that went before. The Hindus give the world an elephant to support it, but they make the elephant stand upon a tortoise. Invention, it must be humbly admitted, does not consist in creating out of void, but out of chaos. The materials must, in the first place, be afforded. It can give form to dark, shapeless substances, but cannot bring into being the substance itself.' Her words fit perfectly the genesis of the vampire Dracula myth created by

Stoker out of haphazardly selected facts and outlandish folklore traditions.

With an unerring eye for the Victorian love of the horrific and the macabre, Stoker transformed the traditionally cruel Dracula into a vampire to suit popular tastes. The fact that in Transylvanian folklore the *dracul* (Rumanian for devil) stories and the vampire myth were *never* mixed together did not deter Stoker from endowing his hero with new traits. After all, Sheridan Le Fanu in his *Carmilla* (1871) created a woman vampire rooted in Carinthian tradition but endowed with the characteristics that nineteenth century readers expected of vampires. Furthermore, Stoker was not writing history, he was penning horror fiction.

As Harry Ludlam, his biographer, notes, having dreamed up a vampire king rising from the tomb, Stoker had to find the right setting for his story. A chance meeting with Professor Ármin Vámbery of Budapest University, a famous Orientalist, attracted his attention to Transylvania as a suitably remote and superstition-ridden region which could serve as a romantic backdrop for his story.

It was an admirable choice. Although Stoker was only dimly aware of it, the memory of pagan religious practices, superstitions and legends still survive in communities, huddled in the Carpathian valleys, that were old when the Hungarian tribes swept down on Transylvania over a thousand years ago. It is a land where the miraculous is held to be as probable as the ordinary, and where the beliefs and superstitions, ancient and modern, of three races intermingle.

Stoker appears to have got most of his ethnographical and historical material from the British Museum Library. In the novel, Jonathan Harker, the London lawyer entrusted with the task of preparing Count Dracula's move from his crumbling Gothic castle in Transylvania to Britain, gets his information from the British Museum where he 'made search among the books and maps in the library regarding Transylvania'. Harker, who is often used as the author's mouthpiece, also makes clear why Stoker finally chose Transylvania as the setting of his story:

'In the population of Transylvania there are four distinct nationalities. Saxons in the south and, mixed with them, the Walachs (Rumanians), who are descendants of the Dacians; Magyars in the west and Szekelys* in the east and north. I read that every known superstition in the world is gathered into the horseshoe of the Carpathians, as if it were the centre of some sort of imaginative whirlpool.'

Transylvanians are also fervent believers—and with good historical reasons, as we shall see—in the powers of human vampires. Among the many superstitions current in the nineteenth century the *dracul* stories, concerned with the supernatural powers of people in league with the Evil One, were eminently suited to Stoker's purposes. Having signally failed to penetrate the folklore traditions of the region, Stoker did not hesitate to amalgamate the *dracul* stories with the vampire element that his horror novel needed and the highly emotive (but unconnected) name of Dracula.

Stoker's biographer fails to elucidate satisfactorily how Stoker chanced upon the historical Dracula. Professor Vámbery's role is vague, and the material adduced by Ludlam, consisting of scraps of second-hand hearsay and disjointed information, does not stand up to critical analysis.

Books on Transylvania, including several guide books† available at the British Museum, could have attracted Stoker to the *dracul* superstitions, or indeed Professor Vámbery might have mentioned them to him. But in the course of the historical research which he is known to have undertaken, he could not have failed to notice the *apparent* link between these and Voivode (Prince) Dracula, a fifteenth century ruler of the Walachian principality of Muntenia, which borders upon Transylvania. Although the *dracul* stories do not derive from the deeds of

* The Szekelys are not a distinct race but the descendants of warrior Hungarian frontier guards settled in eastern Transylvania by King St Laszlo around the twelfth century. Stoker reproduces a nineteenth-century misunderstanding about their origins, which held that the Szekelys came to Transylvania with Attila's Huns some five centuries before the Hungarian invasion.

† E. Gerard's *The Land Beyond the Forest* (Edinburgh, 1888) is most likely to have been one of them.

Voivode Dracula, famed for his gruesome cruelties, Stoker decided to resurrect him with suitably altered characteristics.

In Stoker's tale, Count Dracula presents himself to his London lawyer as a noble Boyar, a term applicable in the Balkans only to the noblemen and rulers of Muntenia and Moldova (now known as Rumania). This would make him a Rumanian, but he also claims the right to the title of the Count of Beszterce, which was historically one of the titles of John Hunyadi, Protector and Governor of Hungary and Prince of Transylvania in the first half of the fifteenth century. This would then make him a Transylvanian Szekely, that is, a Hungarian.

Stoker throws in further morsels of confused historical information, fashionable myths and ethnographic fiction when establishing Dracula's Transylvanian genealogy. ' "We Szekelys"', Count Dracula declares, ' "have a right to be proud, for in our veins flows the blood of many races who fought as the lions fight for lordship. Here in the whirlpool of European races, the Ugric tribes . . . found the Huns, whose warlike fury had swept the earth like a living flame, till the dying peoples held that in their veins ran the blood of those old witches, who, expelled from Scythia, had mated with the devils in the desert. Fools, fools! What devil or what witch was ever so great as Attila, whose blood is in these veins?

' "Is it a wonder that we were a conquering race; that we were proud; that when the Magyar, the Lombard, the Avar, the Bulgar, or the Turk poured his thousands on our frontiers, we drove them back? Is it strange that when Árpad and his legions swept through the Hungarian fatherland he found us here when he reached the frontier; that the Honfoglalás* was completed there? And that when the Hungarian flood swept eastwards, the Szekelys were claimed as kindred by the victorious Magyars, and to us for centuries they entrusted the guarding of the frontier of Turkeyland?

' ". . . When the flags of the Walach and the Magyar went

* The millenary of Honfoglalás, the Hungarian invasion of their present-day territory, was being celebrated with great pomp and circumstance in 1896—the year when Stoker was writing Dracula.

down beneath the Crescent, who was it but one of my own race who as Voivode crossed the Danube and beat the Turk, on his own ground! This was a Dracula indeed. Again, when, after the battle of Mohács, we threw off the Hungarian yoke, we of the Dracula blood were among their leaders, for our spirit would not brook that we were not free. Ah, young sir, the Szekelys—and the Draculas as their heart's blood, their brains, and their swords—can boast a record that mushroom growths like the Hapsburgs and the Romanoffs can never reach. The warlike days are over. Blood is too precious a thing in these days of dishonourable peace." '

Out of this pot-pourri of known historical facts and fanciful fiction, however, certain real historical personalities of the fifteenth century emerge. The Voivode who beat the Turks on their territory was clearly John Hunyadi, the Governor of Hungary. His victory over the Turks at Nándorfehérvár in 1456 stemmed the eastern threat to Europe for a hundred years and earned him the nickname 'Turk-beater'. And the 'ancestor' who fought the Turks can, on the evidence of mid-fifteenth-century campaigns, be identified as Vlad III *Dracul*, who distinguished himself in the battle of Varna in 1444.

The only East European ruler to have had the epithet 'Dracul' —not Dracula—was Vlad III of Walachia,* who ruled the principality from 1436 to 1446. He was crowned by Sigismund, the Emperor of the Western Roman empire, at Nuremberg, and invested with the Order of Dragon, which was created to defend the Roman Church against the heretic Hussites.

The reference to the Szekelys 'throwing off the Hungarian yoke' also reflects historical events: these proud Transylvanian Hungarians, in alliance with Rumanian peasants, repeatedly turned against the central government in the fifteenth century in protest against encroachments on their rights. But, on the whole, Stoker takes such liberties with history that, to find the historical Dracula, one must return to the original sources, and piece together whatever reliable information can be gleaned from them, in what amounts to an exercise in historico-philological detective work.

* Szabolcs de Vajay, a noted genealogist, claims to have incontrovertible proof that Vlad III was a descendant in the direct male line of Genghis Khan.

FIVE

Identifying the Historical Dracula

One of the more promising clues to the identity of the historical Dracula, who was used by Bram Stoker to lend his vampire a menacing air of reality, is a philological quirk. Dracula has a seemingly incongrous, apparently feminine -*a* ending, which might mislead unwary inquirers. Put in the right philological context, however, it acts as a clear signpost to Stoker's paradigm. For the answer to this linguistic anomaly can also elucidate the origins of the historical Dracula.

Although -*a* endings in proto-Latin languages like Rumanian usually indicate feminine gender, in the name Dracula it can be explained by reference with the practice of mediaeval and early Renaissance Walachian chancelleries of adding a genitive -*a* suffix to names, to indicate that their bearers are 'the son of' a person of rank. The German *von* and the French *de* fulfilled similar function,

The contemporary Walachian chancelleries were run, like all other cultural activities, by monks of the Greek Orthodox rite, who wrote in the Cyrillic script. Under the influence of the Orthodox Church and its South-Slav monastic scribes, the written language was Middle Bulgarian. This explains the appearance in a Latin language like Rumanian of a Slavonic genitive which could be mistaken for a feminine ending. But the same -*a* ending is a vital philological clue pointing to the 'son of Dracul' as the historical Dracula.*

Philologists agreed at the Sixth Congress of Onomastic

* Professor G. Nandris came to the same conclusions in his analysis of the word 'Dracula' in *The Slavonic and East European Review*, Vol. 37, 1959.

Sciences* that Stoker's Dracula can be identified without a shadow of doubt with Vlad V, called the Impaler,† though it was his father, Vlad III, who was the first Walachian ruler to be called 'Dracul'.‡ Vlad III bore a cross with a dragon on his escutcheon, and it was this dragon, rather than the Rumanian homonym for devil that was the source of the family nickname 'Dracul'. It is hardly conceivable that a ruler who had built churches and fought the infidels should be named after the devil, a taboo word in Rumanian.

Vlad the Impaler used to sign letters to his Hungarian feudal lord and documents for foreign chancelleries, 'Vlad Dracula'. In the two Walachian principalities of Muntenia and Moldova, which form modern Rumania, he was, however, never known by this name: he was always called Ţepeş—'The Impaler'—while the Hungarian and Saxons of Transylvania, Walachia's nearest western neighbours, referred to him as 'Dracula'.

There are extant, in fact, several documents which Vlad the Impaler signed as 'Dragulya', 'Dragkwlya', 'Dragwyla' or 'Dragulya' pending on which of his scribes penned them. A letter to the burghers of Szeben on the vexed issue of taxes, dated August 4, 1475, he signed as 'Dragwyla, Vaivoda partium Transalpinarum'; another, to his Hungarian castellans in Transylvania, written shortly before his murder in 1476, was signed as 'Nos Ladislaus Dragkwlya'.§ In spite of the slight variations in its transcription, due to the careless and haphazard orthography of written Rumanian of the time, his name was translated by the Hungarian and German chancelleries using the Latin alphabet as 'Dracole' or 'Dracula'.

The name is unmistakable, and so is Stoker's indebtedness to Vlad the Impaler in the creation of his vampire count. Stoker's description of Dracula provides confirmatory evidence of this. Although his biographer claims that Henry Irving, the famous

* Munich, 1958.

† Vlad, called the Impaler, ruled Walachia from 1456 to 1462 and for a brief spell in 1475-76.

‡ Vlad III Dracul ruled Walachia from 1436 to 1446.

§ I. Bogdan: *Documentele . . ., Tarrii Romanesti cu Brasovul*, Bucuresti, 1905.

actor to whom Stoker was tied by close bonds of friendship and business, inspired the author in his creation of the Transylvanian vampire, Dracula's physiognomy refutes this. The vampire, as described by Stoker, bears a strong resemblance to the early woodcut portraits of Vlad the Impaler, as a comparison of the main features readily shows.

'His face', Stoker wrote of Dracula 'was strong—very strong—aquiline, with high bridge of the thin nose and peculiarly arched nostrils; with lofty domed forehead, and hair growing scantily round the temples, but profusely elsewhere. His eyebrows were massive, almost meeting over the nose, and with bushy hair that seemed to curl in its profusion. The mouth, so far as I could see under the heavy moustache, was fixed and rather cruel looking, with peculiarly sharp white teeth . . . For the rest, his ears were pale and at the tops extremely pointed; the chin was broad and strong and the cheeks firm though thin. The general effect was one of extraordinary pallor.'

Woodcuts of Vlad the Impaler appeared in several fifteenth century German incunabula recounting the Walachian ruler's deeds. Most of the woodcuts show virtually identical traits of harshness, and indicate that they had a common prototype. This could well have been the original portrait illustrating the first Dracula incunabulum, or perhaps the more garishly coloured portrait shown to the populace all over central Europe, after Dracula's arrest.

The supposition that one or the other served as inspiration for most woodcuts of Dracula printed in the 1480s and 1490s is further strengthened by the fact that the portrait in Bartholomeus Gothan's Lübeck edition—the first surviving illustrated Dracula incunabulum—greatly differs from the usual Lübeck style of general book illustration, which was strongly influenced by the Dutch masters.* The assumption that it was 'borrowed' from a well-known illustration by another contemporary master can hardly be questioned, as the Dracula woodcut in Peter Wagner's 1488 Nuremberg edition (p. 64) and Hans Spoerer's 1491 Bamberg

* Albert Schramm: *Der Bilderschmuck der Frühdrucke*, X–XII, Leipzig, 1927–29.

Uan deme quaden thyrāne Dꝛacole wyda.

A woodcut of Vlad Dracula from the earliest surviving published work about him, which appeared in Lübeck in 1485.

Ein wúnderliche vnd erschröckenliche
hystori von einem großen wúttrich genant
Dracole wayda Der do so gar vnkristen-
liche marter hat an gelegt die menschë. als
mit spissen. auch dy leút zu tod geslyssen ꝛꝛ

Gedruckt zu bamberg im Lxxxxi. iare.

Very similar, the depiction of Dracula in Hans Spoerer's account, published in
Bamberg in 1491.

Barely distinguishable from the Lübeck portrait is this one from a booklet published in
Nuremberg in 1488.

edition (p. 62), as well as several others, are copies of the same portrait.

It is in fact a beautiful example of early Italian Renaissance woodcutting by an experienced master who knew how to lend his portrait a plasticity even without a hint of light and shade. Whether it is really a likeness of Vlad the Impaler is difficult to say, for the engravers of the time considered it more important to conform with Renaissance precepts on wood-engraving than to render true likeness.

What matters, however, about these woodcut portraits of Dracula is that Bram Stoker could easily have laid his hands on a copy of one of them during his researches in the British Museum Library.

Lesser masters of the late fifteenth century tended to tailor their portraits to suit popular tastes. Dracula's notoriety had aroused passionate interest in the person and deeds of what the early news-sheets called 'this scum of the Earth', and pictures of the Walachian tyrant were shown to the populace on market days. Leonhard Hefft, a contemporary German chronicler of European events, noted in his annals of 1462 that after the arrest of 'Dracole Wayda, who seems to have such a stern and cruel face', by King Matthias Corvinus of Hungary, 'the picture of his countenance was sent practically all over the world as an image to be displayed to all'.*

Similar garishly coloured portraits of Sultan Muhammad II, Vlad the Impaler's great adversary, were also shown at market places in central Europe, and a woodcut of one appeared in Albert Kunne's news-sheet printed in Trent in 1476, on the conqueror of Constantinople. But these portraits by itinerant Italian engravers, pandering to popular tastes, greatly differed from the authentic portrait painted by Gentile Bellini in the sultan's Constantinople court.

The discovery a few years ago of a unique fifteenth-century Dracula news-sheet with a hitherto unknown woodcut of the

---

* Leonhard Hefft's *Chronicle of 1462* (Munich, Arch. No: 26632, f. 495) records: 'Adeo denique visu crudelis et austerus apparet, ut imago vultus sui in universum fere sit orbem depictam/depicta/in spectaculum missa.'

Impaler has shed new light not only on the surprisingly rapid spread of the Dracula story throughout Germany, where the new printing presses proliferated, but also on the source of the Dracula portraits.

The woodcut on the title-page of the news-sheet, printed in Leipzig in eastern Germany in 1493, differs greatly from the portraits in the eight known copies of *Hystorie von Dracole Wayda* printed in the southern and northern cities of Germany in the late fifteenth century, all of which had a common source. Significantly, it also differs in style from the woodcuts in other Leipzig publications of the time.

It has long been suspected, without being conclusively proved, that there also existed a hand-painted portrait of Vlad the Impaler, which served as the prototype for the illustration of hand-copied Dracula stories. The stylistic peculiarities and the very detailed rendering of facial features in the Leipzig incunabulum points to its being a woodcut copy of this portrait, probably painted by one of the refugees from Walachia who knew Vlad the Impaler and whose story formed the basis of the handwritten Dracula pamphlet.

Professor Striedter* maintains that handwritten copies of the Dracula story, in the traditional form of mediaeval monastic 'news-letters', were in great demand and circulated alongside the new-fangled incunabula all over Germany in the last decades of the fifteenth century. As only two of these hand-copied stories survived, the Leipzig portrait provides a dramatically convincing confirmation both of Striedter's theory and of the existence of two portrait prototypes.

The 1493 Leipzig edition of the Dracula story was discovered by chance during the recataloguing of Leningrad's Saltykov-Shchedrin Library in the early 1960s after having lain unknown to the outside world for over four and a half centuries. The four-page *Historie von Dracule Wajda* was appended at the end of a slim volume containing four Latin incunabula of an ecclesiastical

---

* J. Striedter: 'Die ErZählung vom walachischen Vojevoden Drakula in der russischen und deutschen überlieferung'. *Zeitschrift für Slavische Philologie*, Bd. XXIX, H.2, 1961.

Ein wunderliche vnd erschro ckenliche Histori von einem grossen wüterich genant Dracole Wayda Der do so gar vnkristeliche marter hat angelegt de meschen als mit spissen . auch die leüt zu tod geschliffen ze.

This portrait of Dracula, from the recently-discovered Leipzig edition of the story, is very different from those shown on pages 62–4. The style here suggests a much greater degree of realism, in contrast to the Renaissance formality of the others, making it quite likely that this woodcut is very much what 'the Impaler' looked like.

nature and a German-language eye-witness account of the pomp and circumstance of the funeral of Emperor Friedrich III of Austria.*

It was probably bought by a Russian envoy travelling through Germany at the beginning of the sixteenth century, and deposited with other documents in the archives of the Foreign Ministry. The reason for its purchase forgotten, it was eventually transferred to a St Petersburg library where it lay until the last decade.

The six booklets comprising this volume, all dating to the early 1490s, were bound in expensive brown hide with metal clasps, intimating that its original owner must have been a man of substance and taste. The fact that three of the books in the volume were printed by small Leipzig printers working mainly for local consumption, while the remaining three were popular incunabula with a wide circulation throughout Germany, suggests that the owner lived in Leipzig himself.

The catholic choice of religious and secular books gathered in one volume reveals a great deal about the reader—a man who would have wanted the story of Dracula for his library under the cover of 'safe' sermons and collections of prayers. Although the sermons and St Thomas Aquinas' *De arte et vero modo predicandi* could have been useful to any reasonably educated clergyman, the secular nature of the last two German-language incunabula points to a person of wider intellectual interests.

He was in all probability a middle-ranking official reflecting in his interests Renaissance man's thirst for information. The news-letter about the burial of Friedrich III described in detail an event that was of great interest to the whole German-speaking world. The Dracula news-sheet, although it touched upon events that had a special relevance to Germans, represented a novel type of secular literature aimed at the newly emergent European middle-brow readership.

* Ya. S. Lurye: *Povest o Drakule*, Akademiya Nauk SSSR, Moscow, 1964.

SIX

Renaissance Europe's Fascination with the Walachian Warlord

The cruelties of Voivode Dracula shocked and fascinated Renaissance Europe, and were legendary in his lifetime.

The chronicles of neighbouring Hungary and Germany recorded his unspeakable cruelties with the obvious intention of indicting Dracula in the eyes of European public opinion. The annals of his own country described how he killed in their thousands the nobles of his land who opposed his absolute powers, and devastated the lands of his peasants with the scorched-earth policy that he pursued during his numerous campaigns. But they failed to mention that the admittedly terrifying punishments meted out to the feudal barons (boyars) were in order to curb their abuses and strengthen central power. Nor did they stress that, in theory, he pursued a surprisingly enlightened policy toward the peasant masses when he promised that 'nobody shall be poor but all shall be rich in the country'.

It was left to the chroniclers of more distant nations, like the Byzantine Laonik Khalkokondiles to praise his campaigns against the Turks and hail him in 1463 as 'a hero of Christianity' for defeating Muhammed II on the Danube two years earlier.

Voivode Dracula lost the favour of Matthias Corvinus of Hungary, the most powerful monarch in central Europe in the fifteenth century, through the intrigues of the Saxon merchants of Transylvania, whom he incensed by curtailing their trade monopolies and economic privileges in Walachia. The Saxons, who retained close ties of kinship with the other German-speaking countries of western Europe, 'exposed' Dracula's depredations and massacres in Transylvania in news-letters published in the West.

Dracula's hair-raising exploits became one of the main topics of the news-letters—the forerunners of modern newspapers. The descriptions of 'the many dreadful and horrifying deeds by the monstre Dracula Wayda'* created a real sensation. Although in the first decades after Guttenberg printers considered the publication of religious and theological literature as the main task of their craft, the first sheets devoted entirely to news had already appeared in Augsburg and Venice.

Newsworthiness, in a period when news took months to reach out-lying rural districts and was mainly passed on by word of mouth, was not clearly defined, but the arrest of the cruel Voivode Dracula certainly justified the publication of a news-sheet in 1462. The Dracula story came once again into the lime-light in 1476 when, for political reasons, Matthias Corvinus decided to free him and restore him briefly to the Walachian throne.

The earliest of the extant *reprints* of the 1476 news-sheet on Dracula dates from 1485, and from the evidence of the typeface it can be ascertained that it was printed on the presses of Bartholomeus Gothan in Lübeck. The publication of a news-sheet on Dracula in this distant north German city, instead of Augsburg, the first newspaper centre, or Leipzig, the hub of trade routes to south-east Europe and already famed for its printers and book market in the second half of the fifteenth century, reveals the first conscious use of newspapers to influence European public opinion.

For in 1485—the year of the Lübeck publication—King Matthias Corvinus had invested and occupied Vienna, and this powerful monarch, suddenly the centre of interest, was in need of a 'good European press'.

This was achieved by lending the well-known Dracula story a new twist capable of arousing sympathy among the newly created reading public for the Hungarian king. Certainly, if Pope Pius II† had thought it worth while to record the arrest of Dracula in

---

* *Wayda* is a contemporary Hungarian corruption of the Rumanian word *Voevod*—'princely ruler'.

† Pope Pius II: *Pii Secundi Pontificis Maximii Commentarii Rerum Memorabilis,*

1462, then the release of this human monster could be relied upon to capture public interest.

The desired 'public relations' effect was achieved with the help of a new, politically loaded headline and a shrewd post-script. Whereas the original news-letter—two identical manu-scripts of which have been discovered in the monastery of St Gallen and in Lambach—described the cruelties perpetrated by Voivode Dracula before his 1462 arrest, the 1485 Gothan news-sheet has a new heading stressing that his depredations were not limited to Walachia but affected civilised Hungary too.

It reads: 'About a Wild Tyrant called Dracole Wayda who MCCCCLVI Years after the Birth of Our Lord Jesus Christ Carried out Many Terrible and Wondrous Deeds in Walachia *and* in Hungary'.

The new postscript gives the game away by blandly announc-ing that 'in the long captivity in the Hungarian King's Buda castle, Dracula showed true repentance, embraced the true Christian faith and, after his return to his kingdom by the grace of the Hungarian king, he performed many a good deed'. The inference was clearly to be drawn that the Hungarian king, who succeeded in converting the Walachian monster to Catholicism and showed true Christian magnanimity in restoring him to his throne, must be a pious and saintly ruler. As, apart from these two tendentious changes, the Lübeck news-letter is identical with the original one, it is safe to assume that the Dracula story was considered powerful enough to help carry off this public relations exercise. The choice of the printer Gothan for this task by King Matthias Corvinus can be explained by his ability to translate the original Dracula story into Middle Low German and print it in Lübeck for consumption in the powerful Hanseatic cities.

There is further evidence that at this crucial stage of pursuing his central European ambitions Matthias Corvinus made good use of the printing presses to win friends and influence people.* Well

---

quae temporibus suis contigerunt, 1462. (a.r.d. Joanne Gobellino vicario Bonnen, iamdiu compositi, Francforti, 1614).

*Ilona Hubay: *Egykorú Ujságlap Drakula Vajdárol*, Magyar Könyvszemle, Budapest 1947.

ahead of his contemporaries in realising the power of the press, he informed the world in a news-sheet, printed in Leipzig in 1483, of his campaign against the Turks, who were harrying Christian Carynthia at the time. His defence of Christendom was reckoned to draw sufficient goodwill to cover his forthcoming campaign against the Hapsburgs.

And in 1485, the year Matthias Corvinus occupied Vienna, seditious leaflets calling for rebellion against Friedrich III inundated the realm of the Hapsburg monarch. They were printed in Strasbourg on the orders of the Hungarian King and the Emperor was forced to order their sequestration.

The general European interest in Dracula and his deeds did not wane with the passing of the Hungarian King. The printing presses which had sprung up throughout western and central Europe changed the very nature of information and the pamphleteer-cum-printers could not bring out their incunabula on Dracula fast enough.

In their efforts to hold their readers' interest, the printers soon went beyond the style suited only to shock and enrage, and began lending their stories a literary complexion. The use of the then common anecdotal style helped greatly to expand the scope of Dracula stories. Together with Columbus's letters about the discovery of the New World and the French King's Italian campaigns, Dracula's heinous crimes became the favourite reading matter of Europe.

Parallel with the relatively cheap printed news-sheets, an oral tradition of Dracula legends had become firmly established already in the lifetime of the Walachian tyrant, and the south Slav peoples of the Balkans immortalised his heroic defence of Christendom in the songs about 'Sekula Drakulovic', merging Vlad Dracula and the Serbian Sekula Ban into one superhuman being.

Wandering minstrels who entertained at the tables of the high and mighty of European society included in their repertoire of songs, court chit-chat and news of current events, Voivode Dracula's cruelties. Their audiences, not unlike modern horror fans, loved to hate the Walachian and lapped up the details of his hair-raising deeds.

Michael Beheim, a wandering minstrel who sang at the courts of the Hungarian and Czech Kings and at Wiener-Neustadt, the court of Emperor Friedrich of Austria, set to rhyme the tortures and excesses of Dracula, in a poem running to more than a thousand lines. He was much sought after because his songs and prose recitals of current events had the freshness and immediacy of professional reporters.

A manuscript of Beheim's verses, discovered in the Heidelberg University archives at the end of the last century, reveals the great professional care he took to check the veracity of current news stories he included in his repertoire. The source of his stories on Voivode Dracula was a monk called Jacob, who had fled from Walachia to the monastery of Wiener-Neustadt when Dracula turned on proselytising Catholic monks.

> *Da selbst ich michel beham*
> *gar offt zu disem bruder kam,*
> *der saget mir uil ubel,*
> *dy der trakel waida began*
> *der ich ein tail getichtet han*

> I, Michael Beheim, personally
> visited this monk,
> who told me much of the horror
> committed by the Trakel Waida
> a part of which I versified

Beheim, who arrived at the court of Friedrich III in 1462, the year the Hungarian King arrested Voivode Dracula, clearly included in his verse rumours current at the imperial court about the Walachian warlord's cruelties. He tells basically the same story as the St Gallen and Lambach manuscripts—although each is in a different German dialect—indicating that Monk Jacob was their common source. For, in keeping with the mediaeval news-gathering tradition of monasteries, the Wiener-Neustadt friars wrote down and copied out for distribution Monk Jacob's eye-witness account of Dracula's terror.

The fact that the minstrel had personally talked to the refugee monk explains why his story is more detailed than the monastery manuscripts and has the immediacy and authenticity of a first-hand report.

After describing all the tortures, mass murders and other excesses of Dracula in hair-raising detail, he sent shivers of fear down the spines of his audiences by warning them that the Walachian ruler would not spare them either. No one could be safe while 'this greatest of all tyrants of whom I have ever heard on Earth' was at large. For his victims, 'as I have already hinted to you, were all manner of people, Christians, Slovens, Walachs, Jews, Heathen and Gypsies too'.

By reading the sickening list of cruelties to which the minstrel had treated his noble and high-born audiences, one might begin to understand a bit better not only the style of entertainment at civilised central European courts in the last days of the Middle Ages, but also the springs of the fascination of his normal listeners with a ruler who dared to give free rein to man's killer instincts. Beheim himself left his listeners in no doubt, however, that Dracula was not merely a kind of 'Horla', the representative of the dark side of human nature, but a mad psychopath. There was a moral judgment in his portrayal of the Walachian ruler, whom 'it cheered and who derived pleasure from seeing human blood flow'.

The Dracula story was such a success that, apart from those mentioned, five more editions were published in the 1490s in German alone. Dracula became the talking point of central Europe. Leading printers of the time in search of financially rewarding secular stories seized upon it and more copies were printed than of the Bible, the best seller of the century. Hans Spoerer printed it in Bamberg in 1491, Peter Wagner in Nuremberg around 1488, Christopher Schnaitter in Augsburg in 1494, Ambrosius Huber in Nuremberg in 1499 and Matthias Hupfuff in Strasbourg a year later.

The list is even more impressive if viewed over a slightly longer period: pamphlets containing detailed description of Dracula's cruelties were printed in Nuremberg in 1488, 1499, 1515, and

1521; in Augsburg in 1494, 1520, 1530; in Bamberg in 1491 and in Strasbourg in 1500. There were also Alemanic, Hungarian and Transylvanian Saxon editions, and Jan of Puchov translated it into Czech and published it in Prague in 1554.

It reached Britain in 1558, when Richard Eden translated into English Sebastian Münster's famous *Cosmographia*, which included a special mention of Dracula. Another edition, which appeared in London in 1574 under the title *A Brief Collection of Strange and Memorable things collected out of the 'Cosmography' of Sebastian Münster*, could well have been consulted by Bram Stoker in the British Museum library.

Several decades after the death of the Walachian tyrant and the fading of all political issues directly linked to or created by him, natural curiosity about his fantastic cruelties remained unabated. In an age when the acts of Cesare Borgia, Richard III and Ivan the Terrible were common knowledge, this was an indication of the grip the Dracula legend had on Renaissance Europe.

The avidity with which Voivode Dracula's cruelties were read and talked about in the sixteenth century can only be explained by the fascination that extraordinary horror exerts on ordinary people. There were, however, a number of factors which helped to sustain the high level of general interest in the Walachian tyrant's deeds.

More than half a century after Voivode Dracula's death, his cruelties and handling of the boyars were being consciously exploited in Russia for political ends. The Dracula story was originally imported to the newly unified Russian state by Fyodor Kurytsin, the Muscovite envoy to the court of King Matthias Corvinus of Hungary around 1490. In the 1530s and 1540s it was used to justify the autocratic rule of Ivan the Terrible. Some twenty-two versions of the story—*Slovo o Mutyanskom Voyevode Drakule*—were soon in circulation in Russia.

In western Europe politics did not directly intrude upon or change the Dracula legend, but the emergence of absolute monarchs engaged in a power struggle with their mighty barons certainly helped to keep interest alive in a ruler like Dracula who had made short shrift of his own boyars. The Dracula myth outlived both the absolute monarchs and the barons and found equally responsive audiences in later, more enlightened, centuries.

SEVEN

Feast in the Forest of Impaled Corpses

Impaling on sharp wooden stakes was a particularly slow and painful form of execution. Voivode Dracula's passion for impaling on stakes anyone from small offenders to princes of uncertain loyalty and disrespectful diplomats had earned him the nickname of 'The Impaler'.

During his Bulgarian campaign, as the fifteenth century news-sheets recall, he 'burnt the whole country. And all the people whom he could capture he had impaled on stakes and they numbered twenty-five thousand, not counting those who perished in the fire.'

When the powerful Transylvanian Saxon merchants encouraged a faction seeking to depose him and put his brother on the throne of Walachia, Dracula moved against Brasso (Kronstadt) in Transylvania. 'He robbed the St Jacob Church and set fire to the outskirts of the town. And early next day he had women and men, young and old, next to the same church impaled and had a table put in their midst and partook of breakfast with great appetite.'

In trying to strengthen central power and curb the abuses of the exceedingly rich and powerful boyars he invited them, as the news-sheets record, to a feast. 'When the feasting had ended Dracula asked his guests: how many princes the country had had. And he asked them one by one. They said as many as they could think of, some said fifty and others said thirty, but there was none among them who would have thought less than seven. Then Dracula had them all impaled [for not being able to enumerate the previous rulers of their own country]. And they numbered over five hundred.'

Hie facht sich an gar ein grauſſen
liche erſchröckenliche Hyſtorien. von dem wilden wü-
trich Dracole weyde Wie er die leüt geſpiſt hot vnd
gepraten vñ mit den haüßtern yn einẽ keſſel geſotten

'Dracole Wayda' living up to his nickname. This woodcut, published in Strasbourg in 1500, shows him enjoying a meal while surrounded by the impaled corpses of the burghers of Brasso.

Other noblemen were decapitated and their heads were fed to crabs; then the crabs were served up at a feast given by Voivode Dracula for the friends and relations of the executed nobles.

In another raid on Transylvania he put women and men alike in iron chains and took them back to Walachia 'where he had them all impaled at once'. And the rich Transylvanian town of Szeben (Hermannstadt), which had sent envoys to the Walachian ruler to sort out their differences, was sacked while the talks were still on. 'As the envoys returned home they saw so many impaled corpses that it seemed to them that they saw a big forest.'

The German-language news-sheets also accused Vlad Dracula, the Impaler, of 'inventing terrifying, horrible and unimaginable tortures: such as mothers with their children on their bosom impaled together, so that they jerked unto death; similarly, he had the breasts of young mothers cut off and their children stuffed in head first and then impaled together.

'He had all manner of people, Christians, Jews and heathen, impaled sideways so that they struggled and shook and jerked a long while and tore themselves to bits, as if he were the Devil. Then he had also their hands and feet impaled on sticks, and he told their orphans in his own tongue: they had carried out great foolishness. And so he took his pleasures.'

Certainly his inventiveness when it came to inflicting suffering on his foes was terrifying: the chroniclers likened his cruelties to those of Nero and Diocletian.

He forced mothers to eat their children and compelled husbands to eat their wives. The Turkish envoys, whose master, Muhammad II, he suspected of bad faith, had their soles skinned and salt rubbed into the wounds. Then the goats of the royal household were set on the raw ambassadorial feet to lick the salt off.

Most of the early German language news-sheets quote what appears to be one particular incident, in order to establish that Dracula respected neither age nor sex and that he inflicted his cruelties on Christians and heathen alike. 'In Anno Dni MCCCCLXII Dracula took the town of Great Schyldow. He had more than five thousand people, Christians, Jews and Heathen killed off. Among them were the most beautiful women and virgins who, through the intervention of court servants, were saved, and they begged Dracula that he should marry them off in holy matrimony. Dracula then ordered that all the men and women should be cut to pieces with shields and knives as if they were *kraut*.'

He also ordered the building of a vast copper cauldron with a lid which had holes cut into it. Then he put the people in the cauldron, forced their heads through the holes in the lid and ordered the cauldron to be filled with water, 'then a big fire was lit under the cauldron and the people in it screamed and called out in terrible suffering until they were all cooked'.

Some three hundred Tartars who strayed into Walachia fared somewhat better. 'He [Dracula] took the three best [warriors] from among them and had them fried. The others had to eat them, and he said unto them: You will have to eat each other up in the same manner unless you go to fight the Turks. The Tartars were, however, glad to go and fight the Turks.

'And so Dracula ordered that both man and horse be disguised with the freshly flayed skins of cows. The Turks then saw horse and man noisily emerge from cowskins and took to their heels and jumped into a river, and many a Turk drowned; and the Tartars left the country.'

In the German-language news-sheets which were aimed at the west European reading public there is hardly any rhyme or reason given for the Walachian warlord's savagery. They list the cruelties in a deadpan simple narrative in the best tradition of latter-day popular newspaper reporting. But Antonio Bonfini, King Matthias Corvinus's Italian-born humanist chronicler, presents Voivode Dracula in a more rounded and objective light. He had a wider horizon than the German printer-pamphleteers, and the humanist tradition of polyhistors sustained him in his quest for historic truth. Furthermore, he did not have to dwell on the morbid and sensational in order to justify his writings and was not affected by the outcry of tortured Transylvanian Saxon kinsmen.

'It is said that this Dracula', he wrote in his chronicle,* 'is an

* *Antonii Bonfinii Rerum Ungaricum decades tres* . . . *Basilea*, 1543; and *Unger-*

unbelievably cruel but *just* man.' The two characteristics together would, in Bonfini's opinion, indicate that Vlad Dracula, the Impaler was not a madman. His cruelty, though terrifying in its extremism, was tempered by his sense of justice.

Neither does Bonfini pull punches to justify the arrest of the Walachian ruler by his suzerain, although King Matthias Corvinus's envoys had gone to great pains to explain in the courts of Europe that the intervention in Walachia was in order to end Dracula's cruelties.

'In 1462, the King crossed the [Transylvanian] Alps in order, as it is being said, to free Dracula from the hands of the Turks, for he had given to him a relation of his in matrimony. On arriving there, he, I do not know for what reason, nor has anyone else fully comprehended his reasons, arrested Dracula in Transylvania, and confirmed on the throne another Dracula [Vlad's brother, Radu, the Handsome], appointed by the Turks to rule the province, despite a general expectation to do otherwise. He took Dracula as his prisoner to Buda and held him there in iron for ten years.'

Unlike the German pamphleteers of the time, Bonfini did not call Vlad Dracula 'the dregs of humanity', and he did not judge him on account of his gruesome cruelties alone. Bonfini was not unique in this, for in accordance with the moral precepts of the time, there was nothing untoward in cruelty justified by state or religious reasons.

The methods advocated by Niccolo Machiavelli, through which a ruler can increase and consolidate his power, hardly differ from those employed by Dracula. In *The Prince*, which was based upon his many years of political experience in the service of the Florentine government, Machiavelli suggests that when a ruler has a large number of soldiers under his control 'it is extremely necessary that he should not mind being thought cruel; for without this reputation he could not keep an army united or disposed to any duty.'* The feats of arms and successes of Han

ische Chronica . . . Erstlich durch den hochgelehrten Herrn Antonium Bonfinium in 45 Büchern in Latein beschrieben, Francfurt am Mayn, 1581.
  * *The Prince*, O.U.P., London, 1960.

nibal, for instance, 'could not be due to anything but his inhuman cruelty which, together with his infinite other virtues, made him always venerated and terrible in the sight of his soldiers'.

The shrewd assessment of human nature by this ideologist of Renaissance nation-states is reflected in his advice as to why rulers must be feared rather than loved: 'The reply to this [question] is, that one ought to be both feared and loved, but as it is difficult for the two to go together, it is much safer to be feared than loved. . .' Voivode Dracula, pressed by the Turks and Hungarians, menaced by scheming oligarchs and cruel by nature, must have come to the same conclusion.

His devastation of rich Transylvanian towns, from which he demanded tribute as Prince of Fogaras and Amlas under the Hungarian Crown, is somewhat more understandable—though hardly justifiable—if looked upon from the Machiavellian *raison d'etat*. 'And whoever becomes the ruler of a free city and does not destroy it can expect to be destroyed by it, for it can always find a motive for rebellion in the name of liberty and its ancient usages, which are neither forgotten by lapse of time nor by benefits received . . . It cannot cast aside the memory of its ancient liberty, so that the surest way is either to lay it waste or reside in it.'

Dracula's greed and his indiscriminate butchery of the free people of Transylvanian towns, with their charters of rights and royal tax exemptions, proved his downfall, for eventually the Saxon merchants turned the wrath of the mighty Hungarian King Matthias Corvinus against him. Machiavelli, writing about princes just as gruesome and unscrupulous as Dracula, has a word of advice which the Walachian ruler should have heeded.

'A prince should make himself feared in such a way that if he does not gain love, he at any rate avoids hatred; for fear and the absence of hatred may well go together, and will always be attained by one who abstains from interfering with the property of his citizens and subjects or with their women. And when he is obliged to take the life of anyone, let him do so when there is proper justification and manifest reason for it; but above all he must abstain from taking the property of others, for men forget more easily the death of their fathers than the loss of their patrimony.'

Dracula transgressed these precepts and lost not only his throne but eventually his life. For when his suzerain, King Matthias Corvinus, went with his army against the Impaler, his own angry boyars rose against him and handed him over to the Hungarian King.

EIGHT

The Pamphleteers' Tale of Lazy Women, Sly Monks and Insolent Diplomats

In order to break the monotony of the mere enumeration of acts of savage cruelties—and in keeping with the literary traditions of the time—both the news-sheets and Bonfini's chronicle contain typical mediaeval anecdotes about the 'cruel but just' ruler. These anecdotes, less clear-cut in their moral intentions in the German-language news-sheets, are not sheer inventions, for the most common ones have their roots in historically proven events. Some of these still live on, embellished and embroidered, in the oral Dracula tradition in Rumania. Others were acts attributed to Voivode Dracula because of his great similarity to earlier cruel but supposedly just tyrants in Europe.

One of them concerns some proud Florentine envoys who refused to take off their hats to Dracula, in order to show the Walachian tyrant that their ruler was mightier than he—a fairly common diplomatic device in Renaissance Europe.

'Some Italians were at one time sent to him [Dracula]. As they were taken to him', the news-sheets recount, 'he asked them why would they not take their birettas off, and they answered: it was their habit and that they would not take their hats off even to the [Holy Roman] emperor.

'Dracula immediately had their birettas nailed hard to their heads in order that they should not fall off, and that they should keep alive their tradition. And thus he confirmed the latter.'

Another version of the same anecdote, carried in later, particularly German and Russian, incunabula, relates to Turkish envoys. 'It is said that when Turkish ambassadors who came to see him refused to remove their Phrygian hats, claiming that this was not the habit of their forefathers, he had the hats nailed to their heads with three nails so that they should never have to remove them.'

The anecdote came into its own in Russia where, even at the beginning of the seventeenth century, the nailing of the hats to ambassadorial heads was widely attributed to Ivan the Terrible.

The Dutch traveller I. Danckaert, who was in Russia between 1609–11, describes a similar incident in which Ivan the Terrible had the hat of the Italian envoy nailed to his head. C. Collins, the British traveller, who visited Moscow and travelled in Russia between 1659 and 1667, however, claims that the victim of the cruel Tsar's anger was in fact the French ambassador. He also recounts that Sir Jerome Bowes, the British envoy, who also refused to raise his ambassadorial hat to the Russian ruler, got away with it unscathed.

Sir Jerome Bowes was appointed ambassador to Moscow in 1583, and his claim to remembrance mainly rests on his conduct in _ van the Terrible's barbaric court. Milton* gives a good account of his fearless behaviour. Sir Jerome was due to have an audience with the Tsar shortly after Ivan had had the French ambassador's hat nailed to his head. He duly left his hat on and the Tsar threatened him with similar punishment. Sir Jerome replied that he did not represent the cowardly King of France, but the invincible Queen of England, 'who does not veil her brow nor bare her head to any Prince living'. The Tsar, impressed by Sir Jerome's fearlessness, recommended his bravery and took him into favour. But later, irritated by the assertion of Elizabeth's equality with the French and Spanish kings, he lost patience with him. On another occasion, when the Tsar hinted that Sir Jerome might be defenestrated, he told Ivan the Terrible that Queen Elizabeth would know how to revenge any injury done to her ambassador.

A Dutch engraving of the misfortune of the Italian envoy was torn out from a 1700 edition of Danckaert's travelogue† and pasted into the Russian *Dvinsky Chronicle*.

* John Milton: *A Brief History of Moscovia*, 1682.
† *Zeer gedenkwaardige en naaukeurige historische Reisbeschrijvinge door Vrankrijk, Spangie, Italien, Duitsland, Engeland, Holland en Moscovien*, Leiden, 1700.

A common anecdote included in most early sixteenth-century news-sheets, to illustrate the just but cruel ruler's dislike of flattery and craftiness, involves a hypocritical priest. 'At one time there was a sermonising priest in his [Dracula's] country. He admonished the faithful and told them that their sins would not be forgiven unless unjustly expropriated possessions were returned to their rightful owners', a German news-sheet recounts.

'Dracula invited the priest to be his guest and seated him at his table. He cut a hunk of white bread which he wanted to eat himself. In the meantime, the priest took a bite from the hunk and eventually devoured it. Then Dracula said unto him: Did you not warn the people in your sermon today that their sins would not be forgiven unless they returned all unjustly seized goods and chattels? The priest answered: yes.

'Then Dracula said to him: Why are you then eating my bread, the bit that I had cut off myself?'

And he had the priest, who sermonised about other people's unjustly taken goods but stole bread himself when hungry, impaled on a stake.

Another such tale, concerning two itinerant Catholic proselytising monks, is still alive in the oral tradition of Rumanian peasants in Transylvania. It was included already in the very first fifteenth-century German-language news-sheet. 'Once upon a time two monks came to his country. He sent word to them to come to his court. As they came to him he asked one monk in particular what good the people spoke about him and linked with his name? This monk feared him greatly and answered thus: "All sorts of good things are being said about you." He had this monk taken into custody.

'And they brought the other monk before him, and he was questioned by Dracula as the first was. So this monk thought that he would have to die anyway and decided to tell him nothing but the truth, and spoke: "You are the basest and biggest tyrant one could find anywhere in the world; and I have never seen nor heard a man who would have said anything good about you. And this you have well proved on many a person." And then

Dracula said: "You have told me the truth and I will, therefore, let you live." And he freed him and let him go free.

'And he sent again for the first one with the thought that he too would tell him the truth. He questioned him as before; then Dracula said unto his executioner: "Take him away and kill him and impale him in the name of truth, which he concealed and would not admit to".'

Dracula's dislike of scheming women is dramatically rendered in an anecdote which, apart from being included in most Renaissance news-sheets, has, again, lived on in the Rumanian oral tradition to this day. Petre Ispirescu, a Rumanian writer and folklore collector, recorded a variant of it shortly before the outbreak of the Second World War.*

'Voivode Vlad the Impaler had a mistress. Her house stood in a deserted back street of the capital town of Tirgoviste. Even the dogs stopped barking when he visited her. It must have been for some of her sins that she lost her heart to him.

'The poor woman wanted to please him and he received from her all manner of signs of her love. And when with her, his face became a bit livelier. One day, on seeing him more grim than usual and wishing to cheer him up, she dared tell him a lie: she told him she was with child. The woman knew that Vlad the Impaler punished lies harshly but stuck to her tale even after the ruler warned her not to joke about such things: "If it is proved that I am with child I hope your grace will be pleased", she added.

'Voivode Vlad then had the woman examined by the bath matrons. And they told him that she was not with child. He then took his knife and cut her open up to her breasts and said he wanted to see where the fruit of his loins was. There was none. And he left her and she gave up her soul to her Creator in terrible suffering all because she dared lie in order to humour her lover.'

A slothful woman is the protagonist of another typically mediaeval morality tale which found its way into the earliest news-sheets about Dracula.

'One day, Vlad the Impaler saw a man work on the field in a

* P. Ispirescu: *Viaţa şi faptele lui Vlad Voda Ţepeş*, Cernauti, 1939.

Wreedheid van den Groot-vorſt in Moſcovien.

The cruel but just monarch: Ivan the Terrible orders his servants to nail a disrespectful diplomat's hat to his head. (An engraving in Danckaert's travelogue, 1700)

Countess Elizabeth Báthory and her home. Above, the ruins of Csejthe Castle, in the foothills of the Carpathian mountains, where the Countess perpetrated her crimes of Gothic horror. After her death, the castle remained empty for many years; in the eighteenth century it was struck by lightning and burned down. Below, a very rare contemporary portrait of the sixteenth-century Hungarian noble-woman who led a double life, as a luminary of the Austrian Emperor's court, and as the 'Vampire Lady of the Carpathians'.

The Iron Maiden. The picture in fact shows a later reproduction of that famous sixteenth-century inflictor of pain.

Vampire country: a map (1604)

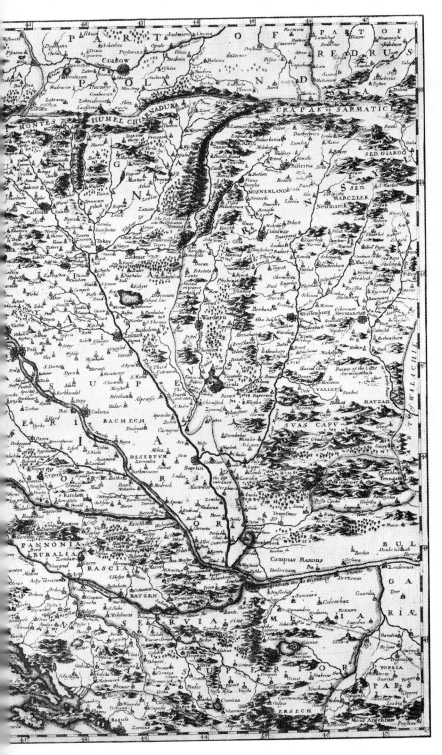

Valachia, Hungary and Transylvania.

This painting, executed in 1896 by the Hungarian artist István Csok, depicts Countess Báthory relishing the torture of young girls. The bloodletting tradition of which her story is a part has shown great durability in eastern Europe.

· The Dracula myth, old and new. Above, the epilogue of the first Russian-language Dracula story, written by the monk Yefrosin in about 1490. Below, Hanns Heinz Ewers, creator of a vampire Everyman in whose veins were mingled the ancient teutonic blood-madness and Nazi Germany's morbid nationalism.

'The bloody terror of Transylvania'—Hollywood's interpretation of the myth, its fangs still undrawn.

short caftan. He asked the man if he had a wife. He answered: "yes". The Voivode then ordered that they bring her before him and asked her what did she do all day long. She said: "I wash and bake and spin."

'He had her immediately impaled on a stake, because she failed to make her husband a long befitting caftan. And he gave the man another wife and told her: she should make him a long caftan, for otherwise he would have her impaled on a stake too.'

The punishment meted out to a sly and scheming envoy who tried to stop him impaling people is another anecdote which became, thanks to the Transylvanian Saxons, part of the European lore on cruel but just rulers.

'An honourable man came to see Dracula', the Renaissance news-sheets relate, 'and he came to him on behalf of the [Saxon] people whom he had so miserably impaled on stakes. Dracula walked about among the impaled people and beheld them. Some [still alive] were also suffering from great thirst.

'Then the man asked Voivode Dracula why was he walking amidst the stench? Dracula said unto him: Does the stench bother you? The man, pretending to be fearful for the safety of the ruler, answered, yes. Dracula had him then and there impaled on a very tall stake well above all the others so that the stench should not bother him any more.'

Perhaps no other single act made Voivode Dracula more popular at home than his standing up to foreign traders who took every Walachian for a thief and, while crossing the country, behaved accordingly. The way he taught a haughty Florentine merchant a memorable lesson is still recounted by Rumanian peasants.*

'Vlad the Impaler was a very severe but just prince. Thieves, liars and spongers he could not suffer. He did all he could to eradicate this kind of people in his country. And if only he could have ruled longer, so they say, he would have cleaned the world from such like misfits, and perhaps he would also have ensured that no similar people should ever be born to this world. But alas, we don't have such luck.

* P. Ispirescu: op. cit.

'In those days, an Italian merchant from the city of Florence came to Vlad's country with a great many goods and a big sum of money in his belt. Having heard from the Turks how they fared with Voivode Vlad, the Impaler he thought that the Walachians [Rumanians] were all cannibals, or, at least, forest brigands. So no sooner had he arrived in Tirgoviste, Vlad's capital city, than he went to the ruler with sumptuous presents and said: "Yours is a Christian country. And in order that they should not say in the West, where I am now returning from the East, that Christian robbed Christian, I beg your Highness on my bended knees to look upon me with mercy and give me some servants for protection while in your country."

'On hearing the request, the Voivode, quick tempered by nature like wildfire, knit his brows and said: "Keep your presents, merchant. I order you to leave overnight all your merchandise on any street or alleyway which seems most deserted and un-noticeable, without guards or supervision. And if anything is missing I will take the responsibility."

'The Florentine submitted to the tyrant's order with a heavy heart. All night he could not sleep a wink. He regained composure only in the morning when he found all his goods untouched, just as he had left them. He could hardly believe his eyes. He went to Vlad the Impaler and praised his country, saying that, although he had been to many parts of the world, he had never seen any-thing like it in any other country. Vlad Voivode then asked him how much the presents he had wanted to give him were worth, and paid him that sum in full. And he said unto him: "Go on your way and tell everyone what you saw in my land." '

The German-language Renaissance news-sheets, however, record that some foreign merchants fared much worse at the hands of Dracula. 'Merchants and other people crossed the Danube [shortly before 1462] with their merchandise from Burzenland, and they numbered VI hundred [600]. Dracula had them all impaled on stakes and their goods confiscated.'

One of Voivode Dracula's most notorious acts was his attempt to rid his country of beggars, professional pilgrims and others subsisting by charity. The news-sheets, out to shock and horrify, duly recorded how 'one day, Dracula had a big meal prepared and invited all the beggars of his country to partake of it. After the meal he had them all herded together in the vast room where they had eaten and drunk the ruler's wines. And he ordered that the building be set on fire and he had them all burnt to death, and he did this because he believed that they were eating up the people's bread for nothing and could not earn it.'

German-language incunabula branded it as an inexcusable act of barbarous savagery, but Rumanian chronicles and the still living lore on Dracula explain the burning of the poor with the ruler's concern for the well-being of the nation. 'In the days of Vlad the Impaler', according to the folklore, 'the idlers had increased in the country to such an extent that you could not turn anywhere without bumping into one. One has to eat in order to live, and they went from courtyard to courtyard begging. They asked for charity, and by charity they lived and did not work.

'When word of it reached Voivode Vlad and he himself beheld the army of poor, most of them brawny, men he began to think: "It is written that man should earn his living with the sweat of his brow, yet these people live by the work of others. It means that they are useless to mankind. It is like robbery. Admittedly, forest brigands would demand your purse. But if you are defter and stronger than they are you can escape from them. The poor, however, take your goods on the quiet, with tearful imploration, but incessantly. It means that they are worse than thieves. This sort of people must be extirpated from my country." '

The popular Renaissance legend about the cruel but just ruler who kills off the beggars of his land in order to spare them the humiliation and suffering of their station and to save the country from hunger, however, is much older than Dracula and his tradition. Similar tales were recounted of several other harsh mediaeval rulers, the savage act being first attributed to Bishop Hatto II of Mainz, who between 968 and 970 AD is alleged to have gathered hundreds of starving peasants into a shed, treated them regally and then burned them to death. Fifteenth and sixteenth-century German chronicles, which first mention Bishop Hatto's deeds, justified the killing of the poor on the same grounds as Dracula.

But the transposition of well-known mediaeval legends and the attribution of others to Dracula as early as the late fifteenth century reveal the extent to which this cruel Walachian warlord captured the imagination of Renaissance Europe.

PART THREE

NINE

The Vampire Lady of the Carpathians

The list of Dracula's cruelties, meticulously recorded by Renaissance pamphleteers and historians alike, is long and exhaustive, but it does not include charges of vampirism. Nor is there any justification for the vampire Dracula in folk legend. Vlad the Impaler must, therefore, be exonerated of vampirism and restored to the rank of European monarchs who, although cruel and savage to a degree, have gone down in history as benefactors of their nation.

Yet there is a strong belief in vampires in the valleys of the Carpathians—the backdrop to Stoker's vampire Count. And, curiously, the undead persons who top the horror charts of Transylvanian folklore are always females. Their attributes include witchcraft, sorcery and the ability to change shape and wander about at night in the form of wolves, owls or black cats in search of human blood.

The popular belief that vampires suck the blood from their victims' throats was widely held among Transylvanian highlanders, even in the mid-nineteenth century, and I came across it in isolated mountain communities well after the Second World War. The vampire stories had a hideous ring of reality for the peasants living on the land which had once belonged to the vast Báthory estates. For at the beginning of the seventeenth century hundreds of young girls were found dead and drained of their life blood in the Carpathians and in the lowlands of Hungary. As Dezső Rexa,* born in the village of Csejthe in the shadow of the Gothic Báthory castle, noted at the beginning of this century, the

* Dezső Rexa: *Báthory Erzsébet, Nádasdy Ferencné*, 1908, Budapest.

villagers had forgotten nothing and still lived in awe of the Vampire Lady.

Official investigations of the murders, conducted by the Lord Palatine, Count Thurzo himself, in 1611, led to the Countess Elisabeth Báthory, a famous society beauty and offspring of one of the ancient European aristocratic families. The Báthorys gave two of the most remarkable ruling princes to Transylvania, a host of warlords and Church dignitaries to Hungary and the empire-builder King Stephen Báthory to Poland.

The vampire scandal, involving in all the murder of six hundred and fifty girls rocked Austro-Hungarian high society. On royal orders, for over a century after the discovery of Countess Báthory's murderous obsession with virgin's blood, no mention was made either of her vicious crimes or, in this relation, of her name in public. Her name was kept out of all contemporary writings, and even eighteenth-century accounts of the Vampire Lady's deeds referred to her only as 'Elisabeth'.

She was, as the judges recorded in passing a verdict on her accomplices on January 7, 1611, 'a blood-thirsty, and blood-sucking Godless woman [who was] caught in the act at Csejthe castle'. It was the first and probably the only reliably recorded instance of vampirism in the annals of Europe. Though the scandal itself could not be hushed up, the Countess's powerful kinsmen succeeded in having the depositions of high-born witnesses and the correspondence of those seeking to intercede on her behalf with the King, the Lord Palatine and the judges of the Royal Curia, deposited immediately in the secret Court archives in Vienna, thus denying access to them for centuries to come.

The trial documents, 'lost' for over a century, were discovered in poor condition in the early 1720s by Father Lászlo Turoczy, a Jesuit priest, in the attic of Bicse castle.* Father Turoczy studied the trial documents and collected the stories still recounted by the villagers of Csejthe about Countess Báthory as the vampire epidemic swept across the country. In 1729 he published a Latin-

---

* In the middle of the nineteenth century the trial documents were finally deposited in the archives of the Esztergom Archbishopric, whence they were later transferred to the Budapest State Archives.

language monograph on the Countess Elisabeth* informing the learned public of her bloodbaths. But he avoided all references to her sorcery and witchcraft lest they reflected badly on the recently reconciled Christian churches of Hungary.

Towards the end of the seventeenth century Michael Wagener attempted to explain in rational terms the origins and causes of Countess Elisabeth's bloodlust. As he also drew on the letters and reports to his ecclesiastic superiors of the Reverend Janos Ponikenusz, the Lutheran pastor of Csejthe, his treatise offered a valuable insight into the Countess's behaviour.†

'Elisabeth was wont to dress well in order to please her husband,' Wagener wrote, 'and she spent half the day over her toilet. On one occasion, her chambermaid saw something wrong with her headdress, and as a recompense for observing it, received such a severe box on the ears that the blood gushed from her nose, and spurted unto her mistress's face.

'When the blood drops were washed off her face, her skin appeared much more beautiful: whiter and more transparent on the spots where the blood had been.

'Elisabeth, therefore, formed the resolution to bathe her face and her whole body in human blood so as to enhance her beauty. Two old women and a certain [fellow called] Ficzko assisted her in her undertaking. This monster used to kill her luckless victim, and the old women caught the blood in which Elisabeth was wont to bathe at the hour of four in the morning. After the bath she appeared more beautiful than ever.

'She continued this habit after the death of her husband [in 1604] in the hope of gaining new suitors.

'The unhappy girls, who were lured to the castle under the promise that they were to be taken into service there, were locked up in a cellar. Elisabeth not infrequently tortured the victims herself; often she changed her clothes which dripped with blood, and renewed her cruelties. The swollen bodies were then cut up with razors. . . .

* Father L. Turoczy: *Ungaria suis cum regibus compendio data*, Nagyszombat, 1729.
† Michael Wagener: *Beitrage zur Philosophischen Anthropologie*, Wien, 1796.

'She caused, in all, the death of 650 girls, some in Csejthe, where she had a cellar constructed for the purpose, others in different localities; for murder and bloodshed became with her a necessity.'

Because a person's character and behaviour are shaped not only by the genetic heritage but also by their environment, one must look outside Countess Elisabeth, as well as within her, to find the whole explanation for her torture and blood fixation.

As an aristocrat, she could arrogate the right to amuse herself in her own fashion without compunction. In abandoning herself completely to her aberrations she did no more than the other aristocrats of her time who pursued with the same vigour their own brands of pleasure.

To judge by her letters, inflicting pain on helpless girls did not clash with her moral or religious convictions. The Protestant nobility extended the Calvinist doctrine of justification through grace to the deeds of the high-born elect, even the mass destruction of virgins. There was, in fact, neither spiritual nor temporal impediment to her indulging her sadistic lesbian fantasies.

Nor did her bloodlust interfere with the major emotions in every woman's life—motherhood and true love for the father of her children. In a strange, almost masculine compartmentalisation of emotions, she appears to have relegated the issue of her tortures to the level the lords of the manor used to approach the 'jus primae noctis'. Her letters to her husband reflect the normal emotions of a doting mother and loving wife.

'My much beloved Husband', she wrote in a typical letter that could have been written by any woman, 'I am writing to offer my service to my beloved Lord and master. As to the children, Grace be to God, they are all right. But Orsika has trouble with her eyes and Kato suffers with her teeth. I myself, thanks be to God, am all right, although I have pain in my eyes. May God guard you and be with you. Sarvar, Anno Domini 1596, 8th day in the month of July.'

She was a highly cultured and intelligent woman. At a time when even the Lord Palatine of the country was barely literate, she could write fluent Hungarian, German and Latin. There were, however, no traces of attempts to intellectualise her predicament, of which, clearly, she was not even aware. Notions of right and wrong did not enter into her blood rituals, compared to which the warped sexual fantasies of the Marquis de Sade would seem little more than the meek libidinous sublimations of a frustrated village parson. She was, by virtue of her wealth and exalted birth, a super-woman, and the peasant girls she destroyed in order to amuse herself did not rate as human beings. Her notions of God, aristocratic privileges and her crude vision of herself fitted perfectly into the social climate of the time.

In the second half of the sixteenth century Hungary was in a parlous state. The tragic consequences of the battle of Mohács,* in which the young monarch Ludovic II, all ecclesiastic, military and state officials, as well as the cream of the nobility, were removed at one blow, became more accentuated. The writ of the government hardly ran outside the chancelleries, and the all-powerful barons took the law into their own greedy hands. Feudalism, unchecked by central authority, reigned supreme in those western and north-eastern parts of the country unoccupied by the Turks. By playing the Hapsburg emperor and Sultan off against each other, the barons were able to maintain their independence.

The causes of the country's decline ran deeper, however, and undermined the social fabric even before the national disaster of Mohács. Sigmund Freiherr von Herberstein, one of the most seasoned diplomatic observers of sixteenth century Europe, provided a graphic first-hand account of the social and moral decline of Hungary.† 'As I am to inform you here on the Kingdom of Hungary, too,' he wrote to Emperor Maximilian, the Holy Roman Emperor, 'I cannot report without sighs and great pain on how this kingdom, such a short time before still very rich, powerful and held in such high esteem, has, with great speed

---

* Hungarian historians refer to Mohács as 'the cemetery of Hungary's national grandeur'.

† Baron Sigmund Herberstein: *Moskouiter wunderbare Historien*, Basel, 1563.

and in front of our very eyes, sunk so painfully low. As all other things in the world, so kingdoms and principalities too have their ordered time span. But this noble Kingdom of Hungary has fallen on hard times not only through God's will but also through poor administration and disorderly government . . .

'[It is] As if the Hungarian empire, after having come in the previous ruler's lifetime to the zenith of power and after his death already began to go downhill, could not carry this great burden [of power] any longer.

'The high aristocracy of the realm, from the spiritual prelates downwards, lived in unbelievable luxury, and each one of them had sought to outdo the other bishops, counts and knights in splendour, haughtiness and wanton desires. Through liege payments and loans, these magnates made the nobles their hangers-on. And through force and their need for these magnates' authority, the nobles were forced to flatter and fawn servilely upon them. And it followed from this that these magnates could, in Parliament, through the nobles' votes and common acclaim, achieve anything or pass any law they pleased. It is a great wonder to behold with what pomp, circumstance, splendour and haughtiness each one of these [magnates] entered the seat of Parliament for the session; they had great many curassiere and light horse to accompany them. They were preceded by trumpeteers, as if participating in a triumphal march.

'When they rode into or left the King's castle, they were surrounded by so many vassals and attendant persons that the streets and alleys could hardly take them. And when they were to seat themselves at their tables there was such blowing of trumpets and whistling in front of the houses that one might have thought one was in a military camp in the field. They sat for hours at their tables, so much so that immediately after eating they had to rest and go to sleep.

'In contrast to this, the King's court was empty and the frontiers of the realm and the market towns were deprived of guards, so that the enemy could devastate them without any sign of resistance.

'The bishoprics and other high honorary offices were not given

An illustration from a sixteenth-century Hungarian almanac. The reader is left in no doubt of the fate in store for peasants who rebelled against their masters.

because of the office bearer's merits, but indiscriminately, to persons whom the most powerful magnates considered right for it. Because of this, justice was hard to come by and the poor were hard pressed. And in the meantime, all the good laws fell into disuse and were undermined, and with every day something new came into being that harmed the common good, and the ordinary man was made to suffer new injuries . . . And in the end there was such disorder and disorganisation in the whole kingdom of Hungary that everyone, so one's judgment suggested, had to realise that this kingdom was in a sorry state of decline.'

The oppressed peasants took to the forests, and pillaged and burned the estates of the aristocracy. György Dozsa's peasant war of 1514 was put down with savage ruthlessness. In retaliation Judge Istvan Verböczy's 1517 Tripartitum Bull tied the free peasants to the land, and reimposed a host of lapsed feudal restrictions. They were deprived of their hard-won rights, and their chances of redress against the wrongs inflicted by their betters were virtually non-existant.

In a society so ridden by privilege and corruption, no one in a position of authority could have been expected to give credence to peasant rumours linking Countess Báthory with the torturing of servants. Parents complaining about their missing daughters were silenced, and the serving maids' tales of blood rituals remained uninvestigated. As whispered rumours of girls' bodies being found drained of blood around Csejthe castle persisted, however, tales of a terrible Vampire Lady who preyed on virgins gained credence not only in the foothills of the Carpathians, but also in Transylvania and the lowlands of Hungary.

TEN

A Lesbian Rake's Progress

Scholars and writers have in the past three hundred years searched for an explanation of the motives of Elisabeth Báthory's deeds. They have discovered many interesting things about the Countess, but the mainspring of her actions has eluded them. She has been called 'terrible ogress', 'human monster' and branded as 'La comtesse hongroisse sanguinare'. Denounced for her necro-sadistic abominations, she has gone down in history as 'The Tigress of Csejthe'. But although her obsession with virgins' blood has been common knowledge, no one has until now linked her with vampirism because of the preconceived notions of the un-dead nature of 'traditional' European blood-suckers.

The mainsprings of vampirism, as Countess Elisabeth's case shows are, however, quite earthy, and there is nothing meta-physical or spectral about them.

Countess Elisabeth, engaged to be married at the age of eleven to Count Ferencz Nadasdy to suit the interests of two exceedingly powerful Protestant families, showed early and clear signs of heterosexual tendencies. She indulged in reckless sexual play in the hay with peasant boys, and at the age of fourteen, while staying at the chateau of Countess Ursula Nadasdy, her future mother-in-law, she was suddenly spirited away by her own mother without the usual retinue to one of the Báthorys' remotest Transylvanian castles. There she was kept in complete isolation on account of 'a contagious disease', and gave birth to a daughter rumoured to have been fathered by one of her peasant playmates. A local woman to whom the child was entrusted left the country for Walachia with Elisabeth's bastard. The Báthorys made her and the child a generous settlement, but they were forbidden to return to Hungary in the Countess's lifetime.

A few months later Elisabeth was married to Count Nadasdy at one of the largest European society weddings of her time, the guests including Emperor Maximilian of Hapsburg.

Countess Elisabeth's young officer husband, greatly favoured by the Hapsburg Emperor who controlled the Catholic Western territories of Hungary, spent most of his time away from home fighting the Turks. His military career went from strength to strength. He became the youngest general to command the border fortress defences of south-west Hungary, and gained the high title of Master of the Emperor's Horse. In 1600 Count Nadasdy was appointed the commander-in-chief of Christian forces in Transdanubia, making him the most powerful person in the country.

During his long absences his bride paid frequent visits to her aunt, the Countess Klara Báthory, a well-known lesbian, who raped most of her ladies-in-waiting, and whose amorous advances to soldiers on guard duty and washerwomen at her castle had made her the talk of Vienna. Her procuresses, well provided with funds, had provided a steady stream of attractive and easy-going girls for her lesbian orgies. Countess Elisabeth must have been very much attracted to the sexual perversions devised by her aunt's fertile mind, to judge by her frequent visits. Although the emphasis at Countess Klara's lesbian orgies was on love-making, the beating of naked, big-bosomed girls appears to have held great attraction for both aunt and niece.

Yet at the same time Countess Elisabeth's interest in men was unmistakable and it went well beyond the mere suffering of her husband's periodic attentions. In the course of her long married life she bore Count Ferencz four children, had several love affairs and, in the early years of her husband's prolonged absences, indulged in sexual horseplay in front of all the castle people with her manservant, István Jezorlay, a man of reputedly exceptional sexual prowess.

But the greatest delight of her life, singularly dedicated to the sampling of physical pleasures and the enhancing of her beauty, was to inflict pain. She was narcissistic and there was a cruel streak in her, which in her childhood had already found a natural outlet in hurting playmates and servants and torturing animals. Her powerful sexual drive rechannelled this innate cruelty and lent it a new complexion. As a young bride, under the flimsy excuse of punishing servants' misdemeanours, she had girls beaten, tortured and disfigured. Her husband, hardened by endless wars, had no real objection to his young bride 'amusing' herself with her servants. Far from trying to suppress his wife's cruel treatment of defenceless girls, he abetted it, and even taught her a novel form of torture known as 'star kicking'. It involved placing paper between a serving maid's toes and setting it alight; the girl kicked and screamed and the pain made her see stars. According to tradition, the young general's favourite party trick was to throw two Turkish prisoners into the air and catch them both on the point of his long swords as they came down.★

His wife did not lag behind in imagination. In one incident she had a girl stripped naked, smeared with honey from top to bottom and left standing tied to a tree for a day and a night at the mercy of forest insects. Girls who broke a plate or displeased the countess were mercilessly horsewhipped, others had their palms and soles beaten with sticks.

Sewing girls who made the slightest mistake in their work were taken to an underground room and cruelly beaten. The room soon acquired the name among the castle servants as 'her Ladyship's torture chamber'. 'If the girls did not complete their sewing by 10 a.m. [the time when the chambermaids began dressing Countess Elisabeth] they were immediately taken away for torturing', one of the Countess's accomplices confessed at the trial. There were occasions when they were driven down like cattle to the torture chamber as many as ten times a day. Four or five naked girls would stand in front of her Ladyship there, and even in that condition they would make her frills and goffer her

★ Pál Kinizsy, a distinguished kinsman of the Báthorys, and also possessed of herculean strength, used to amuse his troops after battles by dancing with two Turks dangling from his mouth by their plaited hair.

ruff, and the lads [doing domestic chores] would see them. . . .
One day, the Lady herself put her finger in a sewing girl's mouth
and pulled it until it split at the corners.'

Dorottya Szentes, one of Countess Elisabeth's wiliest torturers,
revealed in her trial deposition that when her Ladyship was not
feeling well and could not beat anyone, 'she would draw one of
the serving maids suddenly to herself and bite a chunk of flesh
from her cheeks and sink her teeth into her breast and shoulders.
She would stick needles into a girl's fingers and say: "If it hurts
you, you famous whore, pull them out"; but if the girl dared to
draw the needles out her Ladyship ordered her to be beaten and
her fingers slashed up [with razors].'

From the beatings and relatively simple tortures, justified to
herself by the girls' alleged misdemeanours, Countess Elisabeth
soon graduated to wilder erotic-sadistic 'games'. In these, apart
from Dorottya 'Dorka' Szentes, Ilona Jo, her children's nanny,
Katalin Beniczky, a washerwoman, and 'Bald' Mrs Kovacs, were
her obedient tools and willing accomplices. They knew no mercy
and vied with each other and with Anna Darvulia, the sorceress in
the Countess's retinue, in the invention of newer and more
gruesome tortures to amuse their mistress.

Nanny Ilona confessed during her pre-trial interrogation that
they and the Countess 'used to torture girls most cruelly'. Girls
were kept in the dungeon without food or water until their turn
came in the nightly 'games'. After beatings the Countess would
make them pick up a key heated in the fire, or handle burning hot
coins. 'Both her Ladyship and the women burned them on their
lips with the iron used to goffer her ruffs, nose and the inside of
their mouths'. Their flesh was then torn with pincers and razors,
and knives were used to cut the skin between their fingers. The
Countess had a pair of silver pincers which she used solely for
torturing girls.

The girls she liked to 'punish' were usually large, fair and
buxom, and under eighteen years of age. Beating them, she would
work herself into a frenzy, run to and fro in the chamber and
scream obscene abuse at the sobbing girls as they pleaded for
mercy. When her dress became drenched in their blood, she would

change and have other girls brought up from the dungeons, and burn their cheeks and bosoms with a red-hot poker.

On other occasions she would sit in her armchair while the old women beat, slashed and burned the girls, and when the sight of their suffering and the gushing of blood made her wild with sexual delight, she would scream 'More, Dorka, more, harder, much harder'—and then snatch up a candle and burn the writhing girls' genitals.

The inventive Dorka also used to place paper soaked in oil between the girls' thighs and set it alight, and 'punish' their bosoms. After such nights, Janos Ujvary, the Countess's backward, dwarfish manservant, said in his deposition, 'the Lady always rewarded the old women handsomely, especially if they tortured the girls cleverly'.

The clear lesbian character of these nightly sadistic 'games' was emphasised by the fact that there was not a single male among either her victims or her fellow-torturers. Furthermore, a mysterious woman dressed in man's clothing—believed to have been a Vienna highsociety lady of similar inclination who visited the Countess from time to time—joined her in her 'games'. A castle chambermaid once chanced on the pair torturing a girl with her hands tied, who was 'so covered in blood that one could not recognize her'. This whispered rumour was borne out by Janos Chrapmann and Andras Butora, two prosecution witnesses from the village of Csejthe. They testified under oath that a chambermaid who had survived the tortures told them: 'the bloodshedding was carried out by her Ladyship herself, with the help of a woman dressed as a man'. But she could not name this woman.

The close psychological nexus between bloodshed and sexual excitement provides a sufficiently convincing explanation of the root-cause of Countess Elisabeth's perverted deeds. The sight of the flow of blood and human suffering can, to some psychologically damaged persons, cause ecstatic pleasure. Whereas normal people are moved to compassion by the suffering of others, there are those with a certain psychological make-up who are irresistably drawn to torture and bloodshed. In fact, the mainspring of most sexual crimes committed by this category of persons is almost always to shed blood, not to kill. Murder is accidental.

In exploring the psychology of lesbian abberrations—one of which is vampirism—the link between love and pain, the most fundamental in the whole range of sexual psychology, is of crucial importance. Because love was the prerogative of the stronger among primitive men, cruelty and the infliction of pain have become more or less allied to that group of sexual phenomena commonly known as courtship. Blood entered into the sphere of sexual courtship by the same process as cruelty. They were both accidents of combat, and combat, the showing-off of physical prowess, was the very essence of primitive human courtship. This is at the root of that love of cruelty which is, according to Professor Kraft-Ebbing* and many leading Freudian psychologists, so marked in women. For the idea of pain having become associated with courting and sexual excitement, the border between the two becomes blurred and pain comes to be pleasurable even to normal women.

The linking of these two primaeval feelings is consistent with normal emotional and sexual life. The love-bite, however, can easily go beyond the normal confines of sexuality. So can fascination with blood. In their morbid form they lead to perverse impulses, known as 'sadismus feminae', and provide the mainsprings of vampirism.

In the definition of Professor Garnier,† pathological sadism is an impulsive and obsessive sexual perversion characterised by a close connexion between the infliction of pain and sexual orgasm. It fits perfectly the condition of Countess Elisabeth, whom it released from the frustrations of frigidity that she certainly experienced in her love-making with men.

As a rule, the impulses of sadism are less frequent in women because, by their very nature, they represent a pathological intensification of the masculine sexual character. The obstacles in

* Professor Richard Kraft-Ebbing: *Psychopathia Sexualis*, London, 1922.

† Professor P. Garnier: 'Des Perversions Sexuelles', *Congr. Int. du Medicine*, Paris, 1900.

male-orientated European civilisation which impede the gratifica-
tion of these impulses are much greater for women than for men.
But all the same, 'sadismus feminae' does occur, invariably
reaffirming its close link with vampirism. Since Freud revolu-
tionised the psychology of sex, many cases have been recorded in
which women demanded that their partners cut themselves with
a sharp knife before intercourse. They would then suck the blood
from the wound, deriving from the act greater pleasure than from
the ensuing copulation.

The progression from beating, tortures and biting into the
neck and cheeks of girls—the elements of a morbid courtship—
inexorably led, in Countess Elisabeth's case, to bloodsucking, the
perverted consummation of the sexual act.

The sexual urge to torture girls and shed their blood became so
compulsive with Countess Elisabeth that she had special torture
chambers appointed in most of her castles. At his trial her manservant Ujvary, nicknamed Ficzko, who enticed, kidnapped and
procured girls for the Countess, told his judges that 'at Nagy-
Bittse castle girls were tortured in a pantry, at Sarvar castle in the
castle keep that no one was allowed to enter, at Csejthe castle in
the dungeons and in a washroom, at Keresztur castle in the closet,
at Lezeticze in the castle dungeons'.

Even when visiting friends and staying with relations, the first
thing she did on arrival was to look for a suitably isolated chamber
where she could satisfy her passion. At Prince Eszterházy's
Frakno castle, for instance, she used a chamber deep underground
which had been hewn out of the solid rock by hundreds of
Turkish prisoners of war held there in abysmal conditions for
thirty years. In Csejthe castle itself, situated in a no-man's land
where no one, neither the Catholic King nor the Protestant
Transylvanian prince, could enforce the laws of the divided
country, she used a deep underground chamber for her acts of
vampirism.

From there the screams of girls writhing in agony could hardly
reach the surface. In any case, it was not up to the peasants to
question how severely she 'punished' her maids, or to the aristocratic neighbours to find fault with her 'games'. The inhibiting

factors of civilisation, which kept other lesbians with weaker sadistic impulses or latent blood fixations from permanent disturbance, were in the case of Elisabeth Báthory signally absent.

ELEVEN

Elisabeth Báthory's 'Elixir of Youth' and the Blood Healing Tradition

Elisabeth Báthory came from an ancient family tainted by madness, epilepsy and all the cruel psychotic abberations produced by endless intermarriage. Both her parents were Báthorys, one from the Ecsed, the other from the Somlyo branch of the family. She was also very superstitious, believed in the magic of incantations, attended secret pagan midnight sacrifices of white horses under sacred oak trees, and employed a practising sorceress, Anna Darvulia, among her retinue.

Yet her belief in the magic properties of human blood and its use as an antidote to all known afflictions did not stem from superstitions peculiar to the valleys of the Carpathians. It reflected the ancient usage of virgins' blood, apparently still not forgotten in her time in eastern and central Europe, as a miraculous healing agent capable of curing leprosy, syphilis and other then incurable diseases.

The ancient belief, that painful and incurable diseases were punishments meted out by the gods for particularly grave sins, was by no means dead. Because body and soul were considered separate but connected entities, the physicians and priests of antiquity supposed that the illnesses of the body were reflections of the sins of the soul, and this axiomatic belief was greatly reinforced by the advent of Christianity. Accordingly, both physicians and priests, the healers of the soul, considered that to cure an illness they must restore the patient to the state of innocence which he or she had enjoyed before falling into sin.

As blood was considered the very essence of life without which there can be no human existence, the physicians naturally turned to the blood of those in a state of innocence—children and virgins —quite literally to wash away the sins of the patient.

This was an expensive and difficult medicine to obtain. In the Mediterranean basin, where it was used from time immemorial to cure leprosy, it was considered a uniquely royal medicine. Pliny recorded that the pharaohs of Egypt, when afflicted by leprosy, used to take baths in human blood to wash the sickness away.*

Constantine the Great was another victim of leprosy. According to Nicephorus Gallistus,† the pagan Greeks in his court advised the Emperor to take a dip in freshly killed children's blood at the Capitolium. He was by that time converted to Christianity, although not yet formally received into the Church, and touched by the pleas of the children's mothers, and reluctant to spill so much innocent blood, he decided against the traditional cure. In due course Pope Sylvester healed him by 'washing his sins away with Holy Water'.

In spite of the efforts of the Church, the people of the Continent succeeded in retaining, in their superstitious beliefs and popular healing methods, the ancient pagan traditions. Medical science in the Dark Ages was an elaboration of, or closely linked to, the surviving ancient superstitious cures, and there was no real division between the ignorant pretenders to medical skills and the simple village healers. Even Avicenna believed implicitly in the curative powers of blood. He recommended the blood of stallions, bulls, goats, sheep, lambs, stags, dogs, rabbits, doves, frogs and bats as the most potent medicine for a host of illnesses.‡

The affinity between folk healing tradition and medical science was particularly emphasised by the great variety of blood healing techniques practised by the physicians of Europe. The drinking of human blood was believed to be the only effective medicine for dropsy in Rome, and, according to Celsus, in the declining years

---

* Pliny in his *Historia Natur.*/26.1.5/ wrote: 'Aegipti peculiare hoc malum et cum in reges incidesset populis funebre quippe in balneis solia temperabantur humano sanguine ad medicinam eam.'

† Nicephorus Gallistus: *Historia Ecclesiastiae*, Basle, 1553.

‡ Avicenna: *Lib. II de sanguine*, cap. 605, Venice 1490.

of the Roman empire the still-warm blood of murdered gladiators was the standard medicine for epileptics. 'This sad medicine made an even sadder affliction bearable', he wrote.*

This superstitious 'cure' certainly survived intact in Hungary, and must have been known to Countess Báthory, (who, incidentally, suffered from epilepsy) for the eighteenth-century historian Gebhardi noted its common use even in his day. 'The drinking of the blood of human beings is not a mark of barbarity even in our time, for epileptics are often allowed to drink from the still warm blood of newly executed wrongdoers.'†

In mediaeval Europe, parallel with the romantic adoration of gracious ladies and the cult of chivalrous love, there went also a sinister blood cult, deeply rooted in Christian tradition, with innocent maidens as its sacrificial lambs. The lady of the castle, the centre of the feudal way of life, had been turned by the knights into a goddess worshipped with ecstatic love poems bordering on the mystical. But chivalry applied only to women who were of aristocratic birth. While knights in shining armour exalted the divine creatures whose service lent strength to their arms in battle, girls were being murdered for their blood in Christendom.

Some were waylaid and killed without much ado for the miraculous substance in their veins. Others happily sacrificed themselves in religiously motivated frenzy, to gain, through their charitable sacrifice for a sick person, everlasting life. Chivalry as an ideal and the sacrifice of innocent girls to cure sick knights sworn to their worship were, in contemporary thinking, complementary rather than mutually exclusive.

The source of the belief in the miraculous healing properties of virgin's blood lay in a combination of the widespread cult of the Virgin Mary, venerated for her specific condition and celestial power, and the literal acceptance of the Church's teaching of salvation through the drinking of Christ's incorruptible blood. The physicians of Montpelier and Salerne, the two most famed European seats of medical learning in mediaeval Europe, set

* Celsus: *De medicina*, lib. 3, cap. 23. Almeloveen, Amsterdam, 1713.
† Gebhardi: *The History of Hungary*, 1783.

great store by the general cleansing and regenerative power of virgins' blood, and prescribed it frequently for maladies for which there was no known cure.

Hartmann von Aue, a twelfth-century Middle-High German poet who, in keeping with the literary tradition of the period, used French romances of chivalry as models for his masterly court epics, described in considerable detail* the way the physicians of Salerne drew blood from a chaste maiden's heart.

Before beginning the operation for the blood needed to cure a sick knight of leprosy, the physician questioned the girl to make sure that her resolve to sacrifice herself was genuine. He then warned her that if she consented to give her blood either as a result of threats from her parents or from the knight, or in ignorance of the consequences, her sacrifice would be in vain.

Even after repeated assurances from the girl that her resolve to sacrifice herself was firm, the physician continued to test her by describing not only the suffering awaiting her but the loss of dignity before death. For nudity, in a period when beauty was associated with dignity and costly apparel, was a particularly demeaning disgrace, thought tolerable only in connexion with martyrdom.

> 'I will undress you', the physician is telling her, 'so that you
>   stand naked
> And your shame and hardship will be great
> Which you will suffer because
> You stand naked before me;
> I will then tie up your arms and legs.
> And if you don't feel mercy for your own life and body
>   think of this pain:
> I will cut to your heart and tear it out live from
>   your breast.'

When, in spite of the warning, the girl removed her clothes in her eagerness to sacrifice herself for the sick knight, she was ordered to climb up onto a high table. She was tied fast to it and

* Hartmann von Aue: *Der Arme Heinrich*, Middle High German MS dating from the end of the twelfth century.

then the physician 'took up a sharp knife which he was wont to use on such occasions. Its blade was long and wide . . . For he felt sorry for her and wanted to kill her quickly.'

Not all those believing in the magic properties of virgins' blood were, however, as fastidious in testing the resolve of the donor, or indeed sought their consent. Sir Thomas Malory, the fifteenth-century English poet who gave epic form to the courtly ideas of love and the martial world of chivalrous knights, also recorded a typical instance of blood healing. The chivalric notions still current in England and on the Continent in Malory's time had come from the civilisation indigenous to the south of France, via the Norman knights who first shaped the ideas of chivalry in England, who spoke French and followed French customs and traditions. As Malory had spent long years as a prisoner in the castle of the Duke of Nemours, his account of the incident of the lady of the castle whose life depended on endless dishfuls of virgin's blood reflected, without a shadow of doubt, current French beliefs.*

'So hit befelle many yerys agone, there happened on her a malodye, and whan she had lyene a grete whyle she felle unto a mesell. And no leche cowde remedye her, but at the laste an olde man sayde, and she myght have a dysshfule of bloode of a maydn, and a clene virgyne in wylle and in worke, and a kynges doughter, that bloode sholde be her helth for to anoynte her withall. And for thys thynge was thys custom made.'

In Book XVII of *Morte d'Arthur*† Sir Percival, his sister and Sir Galahad came across her castle, clearly somewhere in France, where 'they were desyred of a strange custome whiche they wolde not obey'—giving a dishful of blood.

'So there cam a knyght armed aftir them and seyde "Lordys, thys jantillwoman that ye lede with you, ys she a mayde?" "Ye, syr" seyde she, "a mayde I am." Than he toke her by the brydell and sayd, "By the Holy Crosse, ye shall not escape me tofore ye have yolden the custome of the castell."

' "Let her go", sayde Syr Percyvale. "Ye be not wyse, for a

* Sir Thomas Malory: *Morte d'Arthur*, Winchester MS.
† Op. cit., 1526 edition.

mayde, in what place she commythe, ys fre." So in y meane whyle there came out of the castell X or XII knyghtes armed, and with them cam a jantillwoman whiche helde a dyshe of sylver. And then they sayd, "Thys jantillwoman muste yelde us the custome of this castell."

' "Why", sayd syr Galahad, "what ys the custome of thys castell?" "Syr", sayd a knight, "what mayde that passeth here by shall gyve this dyshe full of blode of her righte arme."

' "Blame have he", sayd syr Galahad, "that brought up suche customes." '

Sir Percival and Sir Galahad warded off the knights in search of virgin's blood. But in true Christian spirit, Sir Percival's sister decided to submit to the custom of the castle in the hope of gaining everlasting life in exchange for her sacrifice. 'So one [knight] cam furthe and lette her bloode. And she bled so muche that the dyssh was fulle. Than she lyfft up her honde and blyssed her [the lady of the castle] and seyde to thys lady, "Madam, I am com to my dethe for to hele you. Therefore, for Goddis love, prayeth for me".'

That the taking of blood for medicinal purposes was no rare occurrence in France in Malory's time is emphasised in the book by the tombs of murdered virgins found by Sir Percival and Sir Galahad in a depopulated castle.

'And when they cam there, they founde nother man nother woman that he ne was dede by the vengeaunce of oure Lorde. So with that they harde a voice that sayde, "Thys vengeaunce ys for blode-shedynge of maydens"!

'Also they founde at the ende of the chappel chircheyarde, and therein they myght se a sixti fayre tumbis. And that place was fayre and so delectable that hit semed hem there had bene no tempeste. And there lay the bodyes of all the good maydens which were martirde for the syke lady. Also they founde there namys of ech lady, and of what bloode they were com off. And all were kyngys bloode, and XII of them were kyngs doughtirs.'

If the 'sick lady' of the French castle, and many others before her, cruelly murdered innocent maids in the hope of curing illnesses with their virgin blood, the Countess Báthory was the first to apply this reputedly magic substance to the most dreaded of human afflictions—ageing. The battle against wrinkles and the uphill struggle to retain her beauty, the eternal tragedy of women unable to come to terms with losing their looks, became her obsession. This quest for beauty and the search for an 'elixir of youth' played no little part in her progression from sadistic lesbianism to vampirism—and mass murder.

TWELVE

The Price of Beauty

The death of her husband in 1604 had a shattering effect on Countess Elisabeth, and played an important role in the loosening of the last vestiges of control over her bloodlust. Her famous vanity was showing signs of turning into a morbid fixation with retaining her beauty at all cost, and her psychological need for flattering admiration, from whatever quarter, was becoming insatiable. Although at forty-three she was still considered a famous society beauty and a sexually attractive woman whose jewels and dress creations used to cause a stir at court, the dread of ageing began to fill her waking life.

She would spend long hours in front of her mirror with the potions, creams, essences, rouges, powders and ambergris pots and change her dress five or six times a day. Dozens of seamstresses were on hand to fit new dresses, and her chambermaids were always combing her long black hair and ornamenting it with jewels to suit her attire.

In the evenings Anna Darvulia used to fill her bathtub with jasmin and oil essences and all the healing herbs of the Carpathians which, she persuaded her mistress, helped to retain the bloom in her cheeks. But neither the expensive Eastern essences nor her many beauty preparations could hide the tell-tale wrinkles or stop the relentless onslaught of time.

In her desperation she turned to sorcery and magic. Although she did not confide her innermost thoughts to her diary, the confessions of her accomplices and the observations of the castle people offer ample evidence of the sudden change in the motivation of her acts. Her incantations and 'games' began to gain the

character of propitiation of the envious and malevolent supernatural forces which, she believed, controlled the course of human
life. Her *religious* belief in the power of these forces to reverse
normally irreversible natural events in the lives of human beings
induced her to seek their intercession. By injuring and disfiguring
a great number of young girls she hoped to please these malevolent forces and thus make them reverse the inexorable processes
of ageing.

Countess Elisabeth also employed the occult powers of magic
that, from time immemorial, were assumed to produce the
required effect by imitating the actual process of life, or its
exact reverse. Misguided by her ignorance, she believed that in
order to achieve the miracle on which she was so set she had
only to imitate certain processes of nature. Then, by a secret
sympathy or mystic influence, the drama which she had acted
out in her torture chambers, would be taken up by mightier
and mysterious forces and acted upon in the required manner.
The fatal flaw in her magic, particularly in the use of virgins'
blood, lay not so much in its assumption that events occur in
sequences that are determined by immanent laws, but in her mis-
reading of the nature of the laws which govern those sequences.

The basic principle of all primitive magic—that like produces
like—clearly defines her savage behaviour as an attempt to
'acquire' the youth of her victims. She applied this principle in its
most familiar form, too: trying to kill her enemies by destroying
their effigies or images. She also made use of time-honoured
Transylvanian magic devices. 'Dorka taught me something new',
she wrote in one of her letters. 'You beat to death a little black
cockerel with a white stick; then sprinkle a little of his blood on a
garment belonging to this person. He [the person] will then be
unable to do you any harm.'

Although Dorka, her evil familiar, would murmur incantations incessantly, divine favourable omens and prepare protective
charms in a special 'magic' room at Csejthe Castle, where
Countess Elisabeth was spending more and more of her time, her
powers to administer to the sinister needs of her mistress were
patently too feeble.

In her battle against the ravages of age, the magic of the looking-glass occupied a very special place. The ancient superstition that the image reflected in water or in a looking-glass is the person's soul and that the malevolent spirit *behind* the looking-glass can take away both the image and the life of the person must have guided her in her search for a remedy.* For she believed that by propitiating the spirit behind the looking-glass, which in the course of the years was taking her looks away by degrees, she could reverse the process and regain her looks.

'Her Ladyship had a little black box in which she kept a looking-glass in a pretzel-shaped frame', Ficzko, her manservant, said in his trial deposition describing the Countess in the critical phase when she was undergoing menopause, 'She would make incantations before it for up to two hours a day.'

The propitiatory incantations to the mighty spirit behind the looking-glass still survive in the fairytale formula uttered by the wicked queen in front of her magic mirror,† and the Transylvanian custom of covering mirrors up or turning them towards the wall in houses where a death has occurred endeavours to stop the spirit behind the mirror from letting the departed soul return as an un-dead apparition.

But neither the propitory acts nor the magic incantations before her mirror helped Countess Elisabeth. In the gloom of her deepening crisis she took the incident with the chambermaid's blood as the long-awaited omen of deliverance, and she resolved to bathe regularly in virgins' blood. She took these baths at the magic hour of 4 a.m., when the dark forces of night were already powerless and the first nascent rays of light heralded the birth of a new day and the renewal of the daily cycle of life.‡

* J. G. Frazer in *The Golden Bough* (1922) devotes a whole chapter to the fears of primitive people of malignant spirits taking away their lives by means of their reflection in water.

† 'Mirror, mirror on the wall, who is the fairest of them all' is a typical invocation of the spirit behind the looking-glass: *Snow-White and the Seven Dwarfs*, Brothers Grimm collection.

‡ Father Turoczy and Michael Wagener (see page 94–5) did not analyse the sequence of events leading to Countess Báthory's decision to bathe in virgins' blood and consequently wrongly assumed that it preceded her husband's death.

In order to guard against discovery, she used an ancient protective incantation written, as demanded by her resident sorceress, on the bonnet of a new-born child stolen from a neighbouring village: 'Gold help me; and you too, you all-powerful cloud. Protect me, Elisabeth, and grant me long life. I am in danger, oh cloud.'

It was by one of those quirks of fate which give rise to blind superstitious beliefs that the day before her arrest she lost a much-treasured and even more powerful incantation written on a parchment which she always kept on her person. On discovering the loss, she hurried to Erzsi Majorova, the forest sorceress. At midnight a new protective incantation was written amid traditional sorceresses' ritual. According to the Reverend Janos Ponikenusz, the chaplain of Csejthe Castle, it read:

'God, help me! God, help me! And you little cloud, too! Give health, protection and long life to Elisabeth Báthory, oh God.

'You little cloud send, send must you, ninety-nine cats when I am in danger. And I order you, who are the supreme lord of cats, to tell the cats to gather from wherever they be now, beyond the mountains, beyond the rivers, beyond the seas. Order thy ninety-nine cats to spread out and bite out the heart of King Matthias, Moses Cziraky, and the Lord Palatine, and to gnaw and tear out the heart of Megyery the Red [the Guardian of her son Paul since her husband's death] so that no harm should come to Elisabeth Báthory. Holy Trinity see to it that it is done!'

A few weeks later, Pastor Ponikenusz, who had repeatedly denounced Countess Elisabeth from the pulpit, was attacked and severely bitten by a band of cats. He recounted the strange incident—explicable only in the emotionally overcharged and fear-ridden atmosphere of Csejthe Castle—in a report to his superior, the Very Reverend Elias Lanyi.*

'. . . On the last day of December [1610] as I came home from the castle and parted company with my reverend brethren, the

* The Reverend Ponikenusz' letter of January 11, 1611, to 'The renowned and Very Reverend Elias Lanyi, most learned in matters of theology, Minister of Bittse, Superintendent of the diocesses of Trencsen, Arva and Lipto counties'.

Minister of Leszete and the Minister of Verbo, I was thinking of my [Sunday] sermon. Soon I partook of supper and went to the sitting room to call my servants to prayer; then I returned to my study to pray even more fervently. Presently my wife joined me and we discussed the terrible and wicked events that had recently occurred.

'Now I do not know what to ascribe it to, but I heard then the mewing of cats from the upper floor of the house. In order to be more precise, let me write the events down in the language I use commonly [i.e. Slovak—the rest of the letter is in Latin]. This was not the noise made by ordinary cats. I went upstairs to espy [the cause of the noise] but could not see anything.

'I said to my servant who accompanied me upstairs: "Jano, if you see any cats running about in the yard beat them to death. Do not be afraid." But we found nothing.

'Then my servant said to me: "Sir, the mice are squeaking in the boxroom." I ran hither but found nothing and said "there is nothing here".

'With that I was about to leave the house, and as I was on the last steps on the staircase six cats and dogs, God save us, began to bite into my right leg. Then I said: "You devils go to hell", and hit them with a stick about my leg. Upon this all the animals dashed into the yard. My servant ran after them, but could not see a single one. As you can see, this was the doing of the dragon.'

The cats whose help Elisabeth had sought and similar familiars played a very important role in the witchcraft rituals of fifteenth- and sixteenth-century Britain too, revealing the common European roots of sorcerers' invocations. Agnes Waterhouse, a villager of Hatfield Peverel, suspected of witchcraft was charged at Essex Assizes in 1566 of sending forth 'a thing like a black doge with a face like an ape, a short taile, a cheine and sylver whystle about his neck, and a peyre of hornes on his head', capable of mysteriously injuring people and cows.

The Queen's Attorney, Sir John Fortescue, also questioned her about her blood-fed cat: 'Then saide the queene's atturneye, Agnes Waterhouse when dyd thye cat suck of thy bloud; never said she; no saide hee, let me se; and then the jayler lifted up her kercher on her heade, and there was diverse spottes on her face and one on her nose; then saide the queene's atturneye, in good faith Agnes, when dydde he sucke of thy bloud laste; by my fayth my lord sayde she, not this fortynyght.' She was then sentenced and executed for witchcraft.*

To the backwoodsmen of the vast Carpathian forests, dragons, were-wolves and cats with terrible powers represented the same tangible reality of evil as the 'the thing like a black doge' to the villagers of Hatfield Paverel. To the ordinary people cut off from the outside world, the huge forests and giant peaks of the Carpathians provided not only a way of life but a source of awe and superstition. Strangely enough, it also influenced the lives and conditioned the thinking of well informed ministers and aristocrats, who could escape to the bright lights of Pozsony (Bratislava) and Vienna.

These forests were no sylvan paradise for the serfs on the Báthory–Nadasdy estates or for the Slovak backwoodsmen eking out a meagre subsistence as woodcutters. Their senses were just as oppressed by the dark and dank forests as their minds were by the fearful superstitions they gave rise to. Facts distorted by ignorance and fantasy begotten by fear were linked in their lore. And about this time, female vampires feasting on virgins' blood were added to the long list of ghostly creatures, malevolent fairies, marauding troops and murderous outlaws against whom they needed the protection of charms and incantations.

For Countess Elisabeth's 'beauty baths' had turned the trickle of blood in her torture chambers into a river, and she needed more and more with every passing day. Darvulia, always on the lookout for new delights for her mistress, initiated the newly bereaved Elisabeth into the ultimate in sexual perversion: the killing of girls and the delight in their dying agony. The final thrill, which she would await trembling and screaming, lent a new twist to her 'games', changing their nature and purpose. Torture for torture's sake and acts of vampirism paled in comparison with the joy she experienced in fulfilling her psychopathic killer instincts. With her own children grown up and her

* Alan Macfarlane: *Witchcraft in Tudor and Stuart England*, London, 1970.

husband dead, Countess Elisabeth disengaged herself completely from the socially accepted feminine roles and became more bestially cruel than any man in war-hardened Europe.

On some days 'she had stark naked girls laid flat on the floor of her bedroom', an accomplice testified, 'and she tortured them so much that they had to scoop up the blood by the pailful afterwards and bring up cinders to cover the pools'.

Her victims were kept in the dungeons without food or water, sometimes for up to a week. Brought up enfeebled and petrified with fear to the Countess's secret room, they were subjected to a ritual routine of beatings, burnings and slashings. Anna Darvulia 'tied the naked girls' arms behind their backs with Vienna rope; they [the arms] turned as black as charcoal. Then the women beat them until their bodies split open', Ficzko said in his confession about the murder routine.

'Dorka did the pricking and slashing. The other, Ilona Jo, heated the goffering irons. Both her Ladyship and the old women burned them with the red-hot irons on their lips, on their noses and inside their mouths.' Then the Countess would tear their skins with pincers and Dorka would cut the huge burn blisters open with razors and delight her mistress with the flow of blood. And as the girls, sometimes two or three at a time, lay dying and the Countess was in transports of sexual pleasure, Dorka would cut their veins open with scissors to drain the last drops of blood for the 'beauty bath' at daybreak. At times the screams of dying girls was so loud that the enraged friars from the neighbouring Augustin monastery in Vienna threw pots and pans at the windows of the Nadasdy mansion.

A Viennese girl, lured to the Countess's Keresztur castle, was killed in an orgy of blood. Another girl, recruited for service at Csejthe from the Hungarian plains, travelled a whole month to the Carpathians and was killed on the night of her arrival. A girl called Sitkey was tortured at Pistyan castle for having stolen a pear, and killed by the Countess the following night. A young servant, who did not stand up well to the ordeal in the torture chamber and died very quickly, was written off by an angry Countess in her diary with the laconic remark, 'She was too small.'

Ilona Harczy, a chorister with a beautiful voice, engaged in Vienna, met her fate equally unsatisfactorily, in the Augustiener-strasse mansion. As a compensation, her procurers brought two young sisters to the Countess, who chose the bigger and more voluptuous looking and killed her on her first night of 'service'.

The usual precautions to cover up her grisly 'games' were thrown to the wind as her mental disorders, of the schizophreno-genic family, rapidly progressed to their final phase. The murders now reflected the ageing woman's primaeval jealousy of young girls with firm bodies. The hope of rejuvenation through the blood of virgins of her own children's age or younger showed, beyond the immediate hopes pinned to its magic properties, primitive emotional processes akin to that, described by Freud, of a mother 'eating' her child.

She even reduced her hapless victims to cannibalism proper in insane acts of 'punishment' for their youth and sexual charm, the two feminine attributes she had lost for ever. On occasions she wreaked terrible 'revenge' on young lads, too, whom she saw looking lustful at 'her' girls, by secretly feeding them with the women's flesh.

'We have heard here [at Csejthe[from the very mouth of girls who had survived the [torture] ordeal that some of their fellow victims were forced to eat their own flesh roasted on fire. The flesh of other girls was chopped up fine like mushrooms, cooked and flavoured, and given to young lads who did not know what they were eating', the Reverend Ponikenusz reported to his diocesan superior at the time of the Countess' arrest.

'Oh terrible feats, oh unheard-of cruelties! To my mind there had not been a worse executioner under the sun [than Countess Elisabeth]. But I must contain myself, for my heart is bleeding and I cannot say more.'

Even while the Countess moved restlessly with her retinue and heyducks from castle to castle, she continued to torture and kill. The hours that she used to while away in the coach-and-six with beating, biting and sticking needles into unfortunate travelling companions now proved too long without the thrill of killing. On one occasion, it was recalled at her accomplices' trial, she went on beating a lady-in-waiting, a noble girl of Dömölk, even as she lay dying in the coach. Her body was eventually dumped by the roadside for the wolves to dispose of.

Countess Elisabeth began showing similar disregard of eye-witnesses on a growing number of occasions, trusting blindly in the parchment incantation to keep those in authority from interfering with her. During a visit to Prince Eszterhazy at Forchen-stein castle she had five girls, one after the other, murdered and hidden in the vast subterranean labyrinth. She even chased girls naked into the snow at Csejthe in view of all the castle people, and watched them as they froze stiff in the terrible Carpathian winter. 'She would sprinkle the girls herself,' Ficzko testified, and they just died. Once even here at Bittse [where the trial took place], her Ladyship, as she was about to journey to Predmer, forced a serving girl to immerse herself up to her neck in icy water because she had tried to escape from her service to Illava and had been caught. She was killed at Csejthe.'

Yet with a strange inconsistency Countess Elisabeth insisted on Kata Beniczky scrubbing down the walls, washing out the 'bathtubs' and disposing of all the traces of blood after the nightly murders. At the same time she used the knowledge of herbs and sorcery of Erzsi Majorova to guard against the men who could have prevented her from having her beauty baths. The Countess herself, as 'Bald' Mrs Istvan Kovacs, one of her accomplices, stated under oath, was 'very deft in poisoning and sorcery. In particular, she employed sorcery and incantations against his Gracious Majesty the King, the Lord Palatine, Megyery and others.'

At least one poisoning attempt on the King was revealed by Ficzko. 'The sorceress Majorova had prepared a special potion, which she brought to her Ladyship, who poured it into a huge kneading tub and then took a bath in it at four in the morning. Then part of the bath-water was taken down to the river to rejoin [the living stream]. Then she took her bath a second time in the remaining water, out of which a special seed cake was baked.' It was meant for the King and the Lord Palatine, who were expected at Csejthe Castle, but some of their retainers who ate of it first became sick, and Countess Elisabeth failed to poison her enemies.

The progressive nature of her psychotic affliction made Elisabeth look for more refined devices capable of prolonging the sexual pleasures provided by the death rattle of girls. In the cellar of her Vienna mansion she had a cylindrical iron cage constructed by a blacksmith. It had huge pointed metal spikes turned inward, and the whole contraption was suspended from the ceiling by a pulley allowing it to be raised or lowered. A big, ample-bosomed girl would be chosen by the harridans from among the seamstresses thrown into the dungeons, stripped of her clothes and forced naked into the narrow cage. Once the girl was hoisted up, Dorka would start burning and stabbing her with a red-hot iron. Recoiling from the burning iron, the girl would tear herself on the hundreds of spikes and eventually become impaled. And Countess Elisabeth, screaming obscenities and abuse in a sexual frenzy, would sit on a stool under the cage and expose her face and wrinkled neck and arms to the shower of blood and drink it.

With her twisted instincts—sexual and psychological—cultivated beyond what even her perverted consciousness could safely channel, Elisabeth turned to new forms of horrors to satisfy her craving. In great secrecy and at considerable cost, she had a replica of the most terrifying torture instrument of the seventeenth century—the Iron Maiden constructed. Built to her specifications, it was shaped like a girl with flowing blonde hair. Its teeth, bared into a smile by the mechanism, had been torn from the mouths of the Countess's victims. Significantly, it was naked, complete with red nipples and pubic hair. It could open and close its eyes like an attractive doll and, at a flick of a switch, would clutch the intended victim standing opposite in a deadly embrace and transfix the person with stilettoes thrust out from its flesh-coloured breasts. Other hidden spikes would pierce the victim's genitals. The blood ran down through special channels into a catchment area, and warmed over a slow fire, was used for the ritual bath at daybreak.

The Iron Maiden was installed in the dungeons of Csejthe castle. Rumours of its existence had swept the Carpathian valleys and were recorded at the time in reports to the King and Parliament. Professor Paul A. Keller, who owns Lockenhaus castle, one of the ancient Nadasdy seats in Burgenland (now Austria), told me that he has considerable evidence to prove that the Iron Maiden was first installed and operated in the cellar of Lockenhaus.

In an astonishing near miss, Bram Stoker investigated the lore behind the Nuremberg Iron Maiden in 'The Squaw', a short story marking his first successful excursion into the nether-world of horror, without suspecting the automaton's link with the Vampire Lady. Sheridan Le Fanu's vampire story,* which awakened Stoker's interest in the horrific and the macabre, was much closer to the real thing. Whereas Bram Stoker regarded his Transylvanian vampire king as little more than jolly good blood and thunder,† Le Fanu sketched in convincing detail the lesbian root of real life vampirism: the first hesitant and vaguely amorous advances of Mircalla, Countess of Karnstein, suddenly degenerating into savage vampire attacks. But in comparison with the sea of virgins' blood spilt by Elisabeth Báthory in search of the elixir of youth, the deeds of Dracula and the blood-sucking of Countess Mircalla look no more than what they were—the inventions of writers of Gothic horrors. Fiction, it must be admitted, was no match for the real-life Vampire Lady.

* See pages 50, 54.
† Harry Ludlam: *The Life Story of Bram Stoker*, London, 1962, p. 107.

THIRTEEN

The Case of the 650 Missing Virgins

With up to five or more girls killed per week, serving maids were becoming scarce in the neighbourhood of the Báthory chateau, the more so as the sorceress Darvulia insisted that only young ones 'who had not yet tasted the pleasures of love' be taken on. Her procurers fanned out through the country ranging from village to village in search of attractive girls.

'Mostly Dorka and other women went in search of girls', Ficzko, the Countess's manservant stated at his trial. 'They spoke to the girls about the good conditions of service [at the castle] ... But women in all the villages were eager to get serving girls for her Ladyship. The daughter of one was killed and then she refused to recruit other girls. I myself went six times in search of girls with Dorka. Mrs Jan Barsony went to engage girls for the castle at Taplanfalva; a certain Slovak woman of Sarvar, and the wife of Matyas Eotvos, who lived opposite the mansion of Zalai, also engaged girls for service.

'Mrs Istvan Szabo, too, brought girls, among them her own daughter. She was killed and Mrs Szabo knew that she would be; yet she continued to engage many, many more. Mrs Gyorgy Szabo gave her daughter for service at Csejthe Castle. The girl was killed and she did not bring girls after that. Ilona [Jo] also brought a good many girls for the castle. Kata [Beniczky] never recruited serving girls, she only buried those killed by Dorka.'

The confessions of the Countess's other accomplices revealed that in fact the number of procuresses was larger still. Dorka herself named a Mrs Koechi, who engaged seamstresses and serving maids from the village of Dömölk, while Kata Beniczky stated under oath that, 'apart from the women who were full-time procurers of girls for the castle, a Mrs Liptai and a Mrs Kardocha also engaged in recruiting.' Some of the eager ones even explored the Jewish quarter of Vienna and engaged several girls for the mansion, much against the tradition of using only strapping peasant girls as serving maids.

The procuresses were mostly elderly widows without any regular means of support, who found the task of recruiting 'serving girls' for the mighty Countess Báthory flattering and the pay generous. The greedy ones and those in the know and without scruples were goaded on by special gifts of skirts, fur coats and, occasionally, gold pieces. The parents were easily persuaded to give their daughters into service at the castle of the mighty widow of Count Nadasdy, and gifts of a skirt, goats or lambs made the parting easier. And so for a while girls to satisfy the Countess's murder lust and provide virgins' blood for her beauty baths were never in short supply.

But the Countess's endless baths could not stop the decay. The wrinkles multiplied, her skin sagged and not even her magic mirror could any longer hide it from her that, like any mortal woman, she too had become middle-aged. She was gripped by despair, and the realisation that, in spite of her wealth, power and aristocratic privileges youth was eluding her, made her desperate. The deep emotional crisis was compounded by the death of the sorceress Darvulia, on whose advice she first took to bathing in virgins' blood. Her whole world seemed to be collapsing about her. The mysterious forces of life and youth in human blood had failed her. Her life, so closely tied up with the belief in the magic of blood, seemed not worth living.

Bitterly dissillusioned, the Countess turned upon Erzsi Major-ova,* who had won Elisabeth's confidence with her potions and incantations and knowledge of sorcerer's magic, and threat-ened her with death. But the forest sorceress rose to the challenge and, showing remarkable acumen, reassured her that it was not

* The widow of the tenant-farmer of Miava, her name is a corruption of the Hungarian word 'majoros' (tenant farmer) with a Slovak feminine -ova suffix. Her actual surname has not survived.

the magic properties of virgins' blood that was to be blamed but rather the type of blood she had used on Darvulia's advice. Peasant girls' blood cannot perform miracles, she told Countess Elisabeth, and suggested that blue blood drained from the veins of girls of noble birth be used in the ritual ablutions at daybreak. In a few months' time the Countess would regain her beauty and the fairness of her skin, she promised. And the Countess, driven literally insane by the fear of ageing, was glad to grasp at the hope of having finally found the true 'elixir of youth'.

The forest sorceress's formula suggested the survival in the Carpathean valleys of the ancient European blood healing tradition recounted by Sir Thomas Malory. Although there was no hope of enticing 'maydens of kyngy's bloode', as in the case of the 'Syke Lady' of the French castle, girls of noble birth were lured or kidnapped by their dozen. The hunt for well-born maids was on and soon Countess Báthory's tubs were once again over-flowing with virgins' blood.

'They [the procurers] brought the younger sister of Gergely Janosi, a nobleman, to Csejthe, Nanny Ilona said in her court confession. 'Two girls of illustrious birth from Veche and two from Chegber were also brought; of the latter only one was killed. They brought one from Polian, too, and Mrs Barsony brought a big and beautiful girl, the daughter of a nobleman, and they killed her too.' According to her reckoning, Nanny Ilona participated in the killing of fifty or more girls of noble birth.

As the procuring of well-born girls along the old lines proved impossible, Countess Elisabeth made her 'talent scouts' con-centrate on the homes of impoverished minor gentry. The mighty Lady of Csejthe herself invited the daughters of lesser noblemen to her castle, and in the winter of 1609 some twenty-five barons' daughters came to learn social graces from the widow of General Nadasdy.

As the murder of her well-born charges was bound to cause trouble and arouse unwelcome interest, Countess Elisabeth accused one of the girl companions of having murdered two others for their jewellery and then committed suicide when arrested by the Countess's heyducks. The fact that the girls' bodies showed terrible signs of torture and were drained of their blood was not mentioned, and no bailiff of the King's could enter the Báthory castle to investigate it, let alone question her Ladyship.

The ruse, however, could not be repeated without incalculable consequences, for girls of noble families could not be disposed of as simply as peasant maids. After the rash torture and brutal murder of the teenage Countess Zichy of Ecsed, the enticing of blue-blooded virgins was becoming daily more difficult. In their desperation Dorka and Nanny Ilona even resorted to dressing up peasant girls in the fineries of murdered noblewomen and passing them off in the dim light of the torch-lit torture chamber as newly arrived lady companions.

The erratic baths in blue blood failed to produce the expected results, and the Countess's difficulties in continuing her acts of vampirism and murder were becoming insurmountable. She had managed to put the Reverend Major, her late husband's chaplain, who had publicly denounced her sins, in his place and had fobbed off the Reverend Andras Berthoni, the aged Lutheran pastor of Csejthe, who suspected that the virgins he was asked to bury had been murdered, with the peremptory order: 'Do not ask how they died. Just bury them!' The octogenarian minister could not stand up to the 'Tigress of Csejthe' and he buried scores of innocent maids, drained of their blood by the Countess, secretly and at night as instructed. Those interred in the village cemetery or in the crypt, under the castle church, were entered by the pastor in the castle chronicle with the innocuous remark that they had died of unknown causes. One entry mentions that on a single night he buried nine girls, all of whom had died of 'unknown and mysterious causes'.

However, to lighten his conscience, he wrote down his terrible suspicions regarding the fate of the nine girls, and hid the note among harmless parish documents in the hope that his successor would find it—and act on it. His successor, the Reverend Janos Ponikenusz, who himself unsuspectingly buried several of the Countess's victims, eventually found the note. It confirmed his own suspicions, aroused by the Countess's order to give a

Church funeral to a fearfully mutilated girl and explain away her death by mentioning in his oration that she had been disobedient and had been punished for it.

The Reverend Ponikenusz refused to bury the girl and denounced the Countess's wicked deeds from the pulpit. Following his predecessor's advice, he also investigated the ancient crypt containing the tomb of Count Kristof Orszagh under the castle church, and found that it contained nine deal boxes with the remains of murdered girls. The stench from the putrefying bodies was unbearable, he noted in his report to his ecclesiastic superior, the Very Reverend Elias Lanyi. The letter, however, was intercepted by the Countess's men and never reached its destination. But after this, as Tamás Zima, a trial witness testified, the bodies of all girls killed at Csejthe were secretly taken to the neighbouring village of Lezeticze for burial.

At Keresztur, in Burgenland, the Reverend Pyrethräus refused to give Christian funerals to the many girls who had died of 'mysterious causes' in the castle, despite threats and blandishments from Countess Elisabeth, who gave the living. He denied communion to the Lady of the Castle, but could not stop the nightly secret burials in the churchyard.

The ministers' exhortations and thunderings from the pulpit did not unduly worry Countess Elisabeth, but their refusal to bury the murdered girls and the increasing difficulty of disposing of them eventually began to tell. Because of her macabre insistence on observing the religious proprieties of obsequies, the murdered virgins were, for a while, buried by student seminarists who sung funeral psalms and dirges as defitted the burial of good Christians. But the Countess's insistence on night burials and the hushed explanations by retainers of the need to bury in secret the victims of a 'terrible epidemic' aroused suspicions of black magic —a charge not even Countess Báthory could ignore. As a result Kata Beniczky, Nanny Ilona and Dorka were charged with interring the girls with psalms and tearful dirges.

In Vienna, rumours and the sudden increase in the number of bodies needing disposal, particularly after the installation of 'the cage' in the Nadasdys' Augustinerstrasse mansion, forced Dorka and Kata Beniczky to dump the bloodless female corpses in the fields at night and then quickly disappear before anyone saw them.

Ficzko confessed to having thrown five girls, killed at Csejthe, into a wheat silo, interred two girls in 'the little kitchen garden by the channel', and two others at Lezeticze churchyard at night. He also helped to bury one girl at Podolia, two at Keresztur and one at Sarvar. But he helpfully added that 'the others buried girls at Lezeticze, Keresztur, Sarvar and Beczko castles and everywhere in their neighbourhood'.

Dorka, too, spoke in her trial confession of murdered maids being dumped in wheat pits or transported to Lezeticze and buried at night. But it was Kata Beniczky, the Countess's washerwoman and chief disposer of bodies, who revealed the confusion into which the Countess was thrown shortly before her arrest by the angry denunciations of the Reverend Ponikenusz. 'They killed five girls (of noble birth), only Dorka knows how, for she was with them,' she told her judges.

But instead of disposing of the bodies in secret as usual, 'they were stuffed under a four-poster in a bedroom and flax was piled on top of them. Countess Elisabeth also ordered that food be taken up to them daily as if they were still alive, although they had long since been dead. Then her Ladyship left for Sarvar and ordered that they be buried under the castle. But I did not carry out the order for I had not the strength; their poor bodies were just kept up there and their stench filled the whole castle. I buried them eventually for the love of God with the help of other servants in a wheat pit at night. Dorka interred one by the channel, but the dogs dragged the body out again.'

This same carelessness and, in the final analysis, confused reliance on the magic incantations of the sorceress Majorova, was reflected in the dumping of four murdered girls in the path of roaming wolves from the ramparts of Csejthe castle in the winter of 1610. The villagers of Csejthe, who were terrified of Majorova's evil eye and had attributed the death of girls found drained of their blood to the vampires haunting their forests, were suddenly jolted out of their apathy. Girls had been dying of mysterious causes for years, and there were rumours that when exhumed several of them had been found to be in the 'vampire condition' and not properly decomposed. There were similar reports from other villages in the Carpathians, and the cemeteries everywhere were decked out with sacred flags and anti-vampire Church accessories. But under the impact of Pastor Ponikenusz's sermons and the discovery of the four naked girls below the castle ramparts the people of Csejthe summoned up courage and denounced Countess Báthory to the King.

Rumours of the Countess's bloodbaths and of the destruction wreaked by the 'Iron Maiden' also reached the King through other channels. The Reverend Ponikenusz succeeded in smuggling the secret message of the late Pastor Berthoni, found in the parish archives, to the Lord Palatine. The statement of the dead minister, coupled with all the other evidence, made the Palatine, Count Thurzo, who was her cousin, act with speed. It could not have been an easy decision. After Christmas 1610, he journeyed to Csejthe castle and formally questioned Countess Elisabeth in connexion with the death of nine virgins recorded in the secret note of the late Pastor Berthoni. It formed the basis of the charges against the Countess, although she was cautioned that the number of girls murdered by her was suspected to run into hundreds.

Indeed her accomplices, arrested and questioned by the Palatine's men, quickly confessed to the murders, pleading that they had acted under duress. Ficzko stated that 'women I did not kill, but I killed thirty-seven girls'.* Nanny Ilona admitted that 'she had killed very many', but would not try to guess as to their number, while Dorka confessed to the killing of thirty serving girls, maids and seamstresses'. Kata Beniczky put the number of killed by all at around fifty. Sara Baranya, a servant and witness for the prosecution, said that during her four years of service eighty girls were killed. But their true number was revealed by witness Jakab Szilvassy, of Csejthe, who had seen with his own eyes 'a list or register in the Countess's chest of drawers, which put the number of girls killed

* In fact, he only finished off some of the badly mutilated girls, for he was not allowed to participate in either the tortures or the ritual killings.

at 650, and that number was in her Ladyship's own hand'. A serving maid called Zsuzsanna confirmed this in her own deposition.

Countess Elisabeth, however, haughtily rejected the charges, and dismissed the confessions of her accomplices as the invention of her enemies. When her kinsman, the Palatine, angrily confronted her with the late Pastor Berthoni's note she admitted that she had ordered the secret burial of the nine girls, but glibly explained that there had been a dangerous epidemic and its spread had to be prevented at all cost. The dear old pastor was too old to take it all in, she suggested. As to the accusations of torture and bloodbaths, she laughed them off. She was far from beaten and she fought back with all the vicious cunning and craftiness of a cornered psychopathic killer. She was not prepared to give up 'the elixir of youth' that held out the last hope of regaining her beauty, the more so as she knew that the Palatine could not arrest the widow of one of the most distinguished Protestant peers of the realm without an Act of Parliament. And she was confident that Parliament, her wealth, her family's influence and her Protestant kinsmen would protect a Báthory against the authority of an upstart Catholic king.

But Countess Elisabeth made a grave error of judgment. The political climate had changed in the country after the peace of Vienna of 1608. The lawlessness of the post-Turkish invasion years was disappearing fast and the feudal privileges and excesses of the magnates were being curbed by Matthias II. The reunification of the western Catholic and north and eastern Protestant territories under the Catholic Crown gave new impetus to the Hapsburgs' anti-Protestant campaign, and Countess Báthory was a prominent Protestant. The shock-waves from the ruthless suppression of the Protestant peasant uprising in Upper Austria spread, with some delay, to Hungary too. Lutherans were in many parts deprived of their possessions, preachers were sent to the galleys. Countess Elisabeth's case was used by Cardinal Forgách, the leading light of the Counter-Reformation at the end of the first decade of the seventeenth century, in his attempt to oust 'the heretic' Lord Palatine from office. He did not succeed in this but deprived Count Thurzo of much of his elbow room in protecting his fellow-Protestant kinswoman.

Parliament, hastily summoned in Pozsony at the very end of December 1610, gave, under the pressure of the Catholic lobby, a hearing to the castellan of Csejthe, who presented the complaints of the villagers of Csejthe, and to Megyery 'the Red', the guardian of Countess Elisabeth's son Paul, who took up the case of a murdered peasant girl. Far from coming to the rescue of the widow of the national hero Count Nadasdy, Parliament voiced its horror at her alleged bestial acts of murder and indignantly noted that she also tortured and spilt the blood of girls of noble birth.

The Lord Palatine was consulting the most influential peers of the realm in search of a face-saving formula when an emissary of the King arrived in Pozsony with the royal order to return to Csejthe and punish the guilty ones.

The official report dated January 7 1611, which was kept thereafter in the secret Vienna Imperial Archives, stated: 'On taking cognisance of this [order], his highness took with him Count Miklos Zrinyi and Count György Drugeth, Countess Elisabeth's sons-in-law, their especially selected servants, as well as Imre Megyery, and left the Diet with a considerable retinue of servants and soldiers, for Csejthe. Already as he entered the castle he could convince himself that the witnesses had told the truth.'

For the Palatine, accompanied by Pastor Ponikenusz and led by castle people knowing all the secret passages, was taken through the vast underground labyrinth to the Countess's torture chamber. There he found a big, fair-haired, naked girl dead on the floor. Her fair hair was torn out by the handful, her breasts cut off, her thighs and genitals burnt, her skin torn to shreds. 'Her own mother wouldn't recognise her,' a horrified official noted.

The walls were bespattered with blood and the clockwork machinery of the Iron Maiden was still wound for long hours of work. Nearby, the Palatine's party found two more naked girls, 'similarly tortured and close to death. And there they found Countess Nadasdy too.' The report added that lower down in a cave officials found several girls who had been held without food or water for her Ladyship's next torture session.

'On seeing the signs of her terrible and beastly cruelties, his highness became most indignant. At one with the counsel of his retinue, he ordered that the widow of Count Nadasdy, as befitting a bloodthirsty and blood-sucking Godless woman caught in the act, should be arrested, and he sentenced her to lifelong imprisonment in Csejthe Castle.

'He also ordered that Janos Ficzko, Ilona [Jo], Dorottya [Szentes] and Kata [Beniczky], her accomplices and helpers in the terrifying butcherings, which they themselves had admitted, should be put on trial, and for their horrifying deeds the hardest punishment be meted out on them so that justice should be done and others be deterred from similar wickedness'.

The action taken by the Lord Palatine of Hungary was, in its intention, not unlike the deterrent punishment meted out to the inhabitants of the French castle in Sir Thomas Malory's knightly travelogue, who were smitten for the 'bloode-shedynge of maydens'. After the killing of sixty fair girls for dishfuls of virgins' blood there was in the French castle 'nother man nother woman that he ne was dede by the vengeaunce of oure Lorde'. In the case of the Vampire Lady of Csejthe Castle, however, the voice of the wrathful Lord and the anger of outraged humanity—clearly heard by the Protestant pastors—was muffled by the stewards temporal and spiritual. Considerations of religion and class privileges weighed heavier than the outrage over the shedding of the blood of 650 innocent girls. Countess Elisabeth Báthory's life was spared. Blood once again proved thicker than water.

FOURTEEN

1611 : A Strange Trial

On January 2, 1611, the small market town of Bicse, near Csejthe, saw a strange trial. Three woman accomplices of Countess Elisabeth Báthory—Ilona Jo, Dorka Szentes and Kata Beniczky—and her manservant, Janos Ujvary, who had merely carried out her Ladyship's orders or anticipated them—were facing their judges. Countess Elisabeth, found guilty of vampirism and mass murder of virgins by the Lord Palatine himself, was not in the dock.

There were eighteeen high judges and sworn jurors, under the chairmanship of his Honour Theodáz Szirmiai de Szulyo, judge royal of the King's Curia. The Church authorities, contrary to their established tradition, waived their right to question or try the accused by an ecclesiastical court, although the charges included sorcery, vampirism, ritual murder and blood magic—the classic ingredients of witch trials.

The King's representative demanded that Countess Elisabeth, caught *in flagrante delicto*, be put in the dock too, but in vain. The Lord Palatine, mindful of the shame that would envelop the name of the illustrious Báthory and Nadasdy families, saved the Lady of Csejthe from the disgrace of a public trial. 'As long as I am the Lord Palatine of Hungary, this will not come to pass', he stated. 'The families which have won in the eyes of the nation such high honours on the battlefields shall not be disgraced by the murky shadow of this bestial female. . . . In the interest of future generations of Nadasdys everything is to be done in secret. For if a court were to try her the whole of Hungary would learn of her murders, and it would seem to contravene our laws to spare her life. But having seen her crimes with my own eyes, I have to abandon my plan to put her in a convent for the rest of her life.'

According to the transcripts, the trial began with the reading out of the confessions of the accused. The depositions of the witnesses were also heard by the court, and then the judges began questioning the accused, who did not deny the truthfulness of their confessions made to Gaspar Bajaky, castellan of Bicse, and Gaspar Kardos, public notary, and recorded by Daniel Eördeögh, Esquire. All they wished to add was that their actions had been carried out under the threats and pressures of Countess Elisabeth.

The confessions and testimonies avoided, however, the Countess's acts of vampirism and bloodbaths. When the King's representative insisted that they be further questioned on these points and on the number of girls of noble birth killed, he was over-ruled by the Lord Palatine, who declared that this was not essential and that he was against drawing out the trial unnecessarily. Nor were Countess Elisabeth's ladies-in-waiting, who knew of her murders and bloodbaths and whose word would have weighed heavily with the noble judges, invited to testify.

After a five-day trial and long deliberations, the judges passed the mandatory death sentences on those in the dock. 'Whereas', the sentence said, 'his Highness Count György Thurzo de Bethlenfalva, was unanimously elected by the Estates of the Realm to the office of Lord Palatine, to protect without fear or favour, after God and his Majesty the King, all good persons and punish the evil, His Highness, not wanting to close his eyes and turn a deaf ear to the terror against human blood and the horrifying cruelties unheard of among the weaker sex since the world began, which Elisabeth Báthory, widow of the much esteemed and highly considered Ferencz Nadasdy, perpetrated upon her serving maids, other females and innocent souls, and whom she extirpated from this world in almost unbelievable numbers, has ordered a thorough investigation of the accusations levelled against Countess Nadasdy.

'The truthfulness of these charges was proved by the confessions of her own servants . . .

'As their voluntary confessions, as well as the ones made under torture, together with the evidence provided by witnesses under oath, patently proved their guilt, a guilt surpassing all evil and cruelty, that is murder, butcherings and tortures most horrendous and assorted, and because these grave crimes must be punished with the harshest punishment the law provides, we sentence:

'First of all Ilona [Jo*], secondly Dorottya [Szentes†], as the foremost perpetrators of this great blood crime, and in accordance with the lawful punishment of murderers, to have all the fingers on their hands, which they used as instruments in so much torture and butcherings and which they dipped in the blood of Christians, torn out by the public executioner with a pair of red-hot pincers; thereafter they shall be thrown alive on the fire.

'As to Ficzko [Janos Ujvary], because of his youthful age and complicity in fewer crimes, him we sentence to decapitation. His body, drained of blood, should then be reunited with his two fellow accomplices where we wish that he should be burned.

'Katalin [Beniczky], as the two women accused exonerated her and on the accusations of Ficzko alone we cannot sentence her, should be kept in jail until provable charges are brought against her.

'This sentence was made public and read to the accused and was immediately put into effect and carried out. To testify to this and in order that such things should not occur in the future, we sign this document with our own hands and confirm it with our seal, and allow the same to be handed to his Highness, the Lord Palatine and released [to the public]. Anno Domini 7, January, 1611, in the market town of Bicse.'

The combined influence of the Báthorys and the Nadasdys worked miracles. Not only was the Countess saved from the humiliation and indignity of a criminal trial, but her acts of vampirism and ritual murders were kept out of the trial records. Her attempts at poisoning and the practice of sorcery were briefly touched upon but never fully investigated. The reference to her in the sentence as 'a blood-thirsty, blood-sucking Godless woman [who was] caught in the act at Csejthe Castle', was a concession wrung by the indignant representative of the Catholic Hapsburgs,

---

* Widow of Istvan Nagy.   † Widow of Benedek Szeöch.

who was more concerned with exploiting the charges for an anti-Protestant campaign than with the susceptibilities of the ruling families of Hungary.

But in the course of a wild confrontation with Countess Elisabeth, who was trying in the meantime to escape from Csejthe to her cousin, Gábor Báthory, Prince of Transylvania, the Palatine left no doubt as to his determination to have her punished. 'You, Elisabeth, are like a wild animal', he told her in the presence of the representatives of the Estates of the Realm and her powerful relations. 'You are in the last months of your life. You do not deserve to breathe the air on Earth, nor to see the light of the Lord. You shall disappear from this world and shall never reappear in it again. The shadows will envelop you and you will find time to repent your bestial life. I condemn you, Lady of Csejthe, to lifelong imprisonment in your own castle.'

Considering the public torture and execution of Countess Elisabeth's simple-minded accomplices, lifelong imprisonment in her own castle was not exactly a severe punishment for her Ladyship. It saved her family from disgrace, however, and the Lord Palatine from having to have a Báthory sentenced to death by decapitation—the only possible punishment under the law for the murder of well-born persons.

Countess Elisabeth was beside herself with rage and indignation. She protested violently against her incarceration in Csejthe castle, and repeatedly reproached the Palatine for failing to 'defend her honour'. She also warned him of 'the dire consequences' of his 'illegal action' against the widow of a premier peer, and demanded her immediate and unconditional release. These were no empty threats, for she knew that her kinsmen and relations were doing their utmost to save her.

Morbid to the end, she also reproached the Reverend Ponikenusz, when he went to the castle with other ministers to offer Christian solace to her, for being instrumental in her incarceration. Far from showing repentence for her deeds, she told the clergymen that 'without any doubt the pastor of Csejthe, who castigated me in his every sermon' must bear the blame for her captivity.

The pastor, mindful of the threat posed by the angry Báthory kinsmen, abjectly excused himself to the Countess. 'I only spread God's word, and if ever your conscience pricked you, Your Ladyship, I am not to blame for it, for I never named you by name,' he told her. But the Countess, as he explained in his report to his ecclesiastical superior,* remained adamant: 'For this, she declared 'you must die first, then Squire Megyery. For the pair of you are the cause of my bitter captivity. Don't you think that there will be trouble because of this? There is already an uprising afoot east of the river Tisza, and soon the Prince of Transylvania will be here with his troops to avenge the injustice suffered by me.'

Sensibly, the Reverend Ponikenusz asked his brother minister to pray for him—'for I have many enemies'—and begged him to intercede with the Lord Palatine on his behalf so that 'he should not neglect to protect me, should my fate take a turn for the worse'.

In the meantime, the Countess's relations began an unparallelled campaign to save her from being put on trial, as demanded by the King, who was outraged that 'the guilty woman responsible for the death of three hundred [sic] girls and women born into noble and peasant families'† had escaped the public executioner's axe.

In the weeks following the sensational revelations at the Bicse trial, Countess Elisabeth's mighty relations did all in their power to pervert the course of justice. Some lobbied all amenable members of Parliament, the King's Curia, and the supreme court. Others bombarded the Lord Palatine with letters pleading that he save the family honour and the blameless names of the Báthorys and Nadasdys.

Count Miklos Zrinyi, one of the legendary heroes of the anti-Turkish campaigns, and son-in-law of Countess Elisabeth, was among the first ones to write to the Palatine. He thanked him profusely for his 'kinsman-like goodwill', and implored him to prevent the King from putting his mother-in-law on trial.‡

* Pastor Ponikenusz's letter to the Very Reverend Elias Lanyi, dated Csejthe, January 11, 1611.

† King Matthias II's letter to Palatine Thurzo, dated Vienna, January 14, 1611.

‡ Count Miklos Zrinyi's letter to the Lord Palatine, dated Csaktornya, February 12, 1611.

'. . . I have received and understood your Highness's letter,' Zrinyi wrote, 'as well as the copies of His Majesty's letter to your Highness and your reply to it. And although I am suffering with a hardened heart the bitter and miserable condition in which my mother [in-law] Countess Nadasdy finds herself at present, nevertheless I wish, if comparing her terrible, hair-raising and frightful acts to the present punishiment meted out by your Highness, to choose the lesser of the two evils:

'And that is that your Highness did decree, which was aimed at our common good, the saving of our honour and the elimination of the disgrace facing us, rather than letting come to pass what His Majesty outlined in his letter to your Highness. For if that were to pass it would be better for all of us to die and, together with her kith and kin and their children, crumble to dust. We would rather choose that than hear the punishment pronounced [in a court] for her patently terrible and ugly tortures.

'But your Highness, being kind, kinsman-like and guided by good will, also wishing to prevent this disgrace befalling us, has found the right solution to avoid it by imprisoning her in perpetuity; and this also prevents her punishment disgracing us all and the memory of her pious and heroic husband. We shall be unable to repay your Highness's pious and kinsman-like action to our dying day. Indeed, we shall, with all our might, endeavour to show even a small fraction of our gratitude.

'Nevertheless, we now want to ask your Highness to intercede for my mother [in-law] with His Majesty the King and divert him from meting out the great punishment that he had resolved to pass on her, and to make him be satisfied with the sentence your Highness had passed on her. Please, make [the King] forgo the punishment provided by the law, for your Highness can, without doubt, envisage the extent of the disgrace and the magnitude of the harm that would befall all of us. After God, we place our hope in your Highness and trust that you will plead for us with good result with His Majesty, and that even after this you will be mindful of our interests.'

Count Pál Nadasdy, Elisabeth's son, also wrote a letter to the Lord Palatine, asking him, on the strength of their kinship, to do his utmost to stop the King from having his mother punished 'in accordance with the law'. Couched in just as straight forward a style as that of his brother-in-law, the letter argued that putting her on trial would serve no other purpose than bringing 'eternal disgrace' upon the family. Cleverly it also pointed out that the King's Exchequer would not, as was usual in such cases, benefit from the trial because his mother had shared out all her lands, castles and villages among her children years before her arrest. The logic of his arguments and the drift of his pleas for saving the honour of the family were not impaired by notions of natural justice.

The attempts to sway the opinion of the Hungarian Parliament failed, and in the spring of 1611 it informed the King of its displeasure over the unpardonable leniency shown by the Lord Palatine in the case of Countess Elisabeth Báthory. Their anger was, however, not entirely prompted by the blatant disregard for the country's laws or the crude confirmation of the privileges of the high aristocracy. Religious antagonism appears to have loomed large in the minds of members of the noble Diet as the country, like the rest of Europe, was inexorably sliding into the quagmire of the Thirty Years War.

But the majority of the Royal Hungarian Camera, whose partiality was secured by the tireless Báthory kinsmen, came out in support of the Lord Palatine's decision to save Countess Elisabeth from the executioner's axe. Their advisory letter to the King, representing the opinion of the supreme legal authority of the country, finally swayed the Monarch's determination to let justice take its course.

The letter,* signed by the learned and influential secretaries of the Royal Camera and Council, reasoned that no one was to gain from the public trial of Countess Elisabeth. It hinted at the legal pitfalls the prosecution would face with the unproved case of murder of well-born girls, and emphasised that even if this were to be proved His Majesty's Exchequer could not hope for more than one-third of the estate of a person sentenced to decapitation.

* Letter to King Matthias II by Judges Tamás Vizkelety and Ferencz Lorant, dated Pozsony, March 31, 1611.

Furthermore, 'in the case of simple murder, i.e. of persons of lowly birth, which is a punishable offence, as well as in the case of murder of noble persons, which is a capital offence punishable by Your Majesty's Curia by decapitation, it is not the state prosecutor's duty to sue but that of the interested parties; therefore, it is feared that the prosecution, in the case of an out-of-court settlement with the victims' relations, would find itself excluded from the proceedings'.

The validity of this fine legal point was affirmed by 'virtually all of Your Majesty's judges and jurors of the Royal Curia', the letter informed King Matthias and proceeded to convince him of his duties towards such loyal supporters of the Hapsburg cause as the Báthorys and Nadasdys. 'It is left to Your Majesty's pleasure', it added, 'whether further proceedings should be instituted against the above named Lady with a view to decapitation, or the present sentence of imprisonment in perpetuity be left standing and confirmed, the latter being recommended by the useful and faithful service of her Ladyship's deceased husband, and their daughters' service to Your Majesty, one of whom is married to Miklos Zrinyi, the other to György Homonnay, both Barons of the Realm and faithful and useful servants of Your Majesty.'

On the King's instructions the Royal Curia then confirmed the Lord Palatine's sentence on Countess Báthory. Workmen walled in the windows and doors, and as the Lady of the Castle was immured in a small room with only a food hatch connecting her to the outside world, four gibbets were erected at the four corners of the Gothic castle to remind the village people and to inform travellers that justice was done in Csejthe Castle. And justice it was, after a fashion.

As darkness was closing in on the Vampire Lady, the Palatine performed yet another signal favour to Protestantism—and to the Báthorys. Instead of depositing the trial documents in the court archives, he quietly left them in the attic of his Bicse castle, where they stayed forgotten and at the mercy of rats and leaking roofs until Father Turoczy discovered them in the 1720s.

After three and a half years of living death in her vast, icy tomb in the Carpathians, the Countess died. The brief surviving report of a contemporary chronicler, István Krapinai, could be the Vampire Lady's epitaph: 'Elizabeth Báthory, widow of Count Ferencz Nadasdy, His Majesty's Chief Master of Horse, who was notorious for her murders, died imprisoned at Csejthe castle on August 14th, 1614, suddenly and without a crucifix and without light.'

PART FOUR

FIFTEEN

Russia: Ivan the Terrible and the Justification of Despotism

The incalculable strength of a myth that captures popular imagin-ation is graphically illustrated by the exploitation of the Dracula story to political ends in societies of very different social and religious orders. Through the centuries the Dracula myth has proved much more lasting than the memory of the Walachian ruler who inspired it.

A central European Dracula news-sheet first reached Muscovy several decades after Vlad the Impaler's death. The ruler of that country, Ivan III,* was engaged in a ruthless struggle to unite the East Slavs, now freed from the yoke of the Tartars, into a Russian national state. He was also fired by religious mania. His hatred of all things Western, and 'heretic Catholicism' in particular, was boundless, and he saw Orthodox Moscow as 'the sole guardian of the truth of Christ'. Under him, the first Russian-language Dracula story, *Povesty o Mutyanskom* [Muntyanskom] *Voyevode Drakule*† was written by a monk in the Byelo-Ozero monastery. It became a powerful instrument in the hands of Muscovite despotic theocracy.

The political role played by the Dracula myth in Russia was almost unbelievably powerful. This was due to the fact that it was the first secular work with a contemporary political message to be written in that isolated theocratic state just embarking on the process of secularisation. It was indeed a classical case of a malle-able story being boosted to legendary proportions in order to fulfil a pressing social need.

* 1462–1505.   † Kirilo-Byeloozersky MS No. II/1088, from around 1490.

An epilogue added to the seventeen episodes in the story condemned Dracula for abandoning the true Orthodox faith and for embracing Catholicism while the prisoner of the Hungarian King in Buda. But the injection of direct politico-religious issues into the imported Dracula story was to illustrate the major problems confronting Muscovy. Apart from religion, public attention was focused on the moral issues of autocratic power based on terror, and naturally the *Povesty* fully reflects this major preoccupation of the Russians. Dracula's cruelties, put in the right perspective, were more important to the apologists of despotic rule than the Walachian ruler himself, and accordingly the story is centred around his deeds rather than his person. Already in the 1490s the myth was taking over from the man.

Ivan III married Sophia Paleologue, the niece of the last Byzantine emperor, and a lady of considerable political astuteness with her own notions of the ruler's God-given power. Ivan soon assumed the title of Samoderzhets,* or Autocrat, and justified his despotic rule through the divine source of his power. The Russian Orthodox Church, newly weaned from the Greek mother Church used the Byzantine idea of 'the sacred mission of the imperial power' in its attempt to lend doctrinaire support to the sanctity of state power.

In the void created by the fall of Byzantium to the Turks, Moscow laid claim to the spiritual guidance of the Christian world. As the interests of church and state became, for a while, identical, the fight against 'heretic Catholicism' became the focal point of Russia's new-found universal mission.

Starets Philoteus, a late fifteenth-century Russian ecclesiastic, provided the most powerful vehicle for the expansionist autocratic state by declaring Moscow the 'Third Rome'. Since the first two Romes—sinful Rome and occupied Byzantium—had lost the keys of St Peter, he reasoned, the Russian Orthodox Church must consider itself the sole guardian of the truth of Christ. The 'Third Rome' could only be in Russia because 'the pulse of history beats only in the relationship between God and the "chosen people"'. That the Russians were God's 'chosen people'

* The title is a calque of the Greek αὐτόκρατης.

was self-evident to him because only Holy Russia preserved the purity of the original Christian faith. Certain eschatological forebodings, then current in Russia, lent further support to the notion of Moscow being the 'Third Rome' because the end of the world would prevent the formation of a Fourth.

Since there was no clear distinction between matters temporal and spiritual, the Orthodox clergy's expectation was that the idea of Moscow as the 'Third Rome' would pave the way to the establishment of Christ's earthly empire under the tutelage of the Russian Church. Although the religious ambitions of the entwined Russian church and state were, under Ivan III, kept very much in the foreground, the autocratic state used both the philosophy and organization of the church to further its political ends.

In this moral climate, Dracula's acts of barbarous cruelty must have seemed the perfected expression of Byzantine absolutism. He was introduced to the Russian reader in a fashion that at once established his religious credentials and indicated the import of his actions. 'In the land of the Mutyan [Walachia] there was a monarch of Greek Christian persuasion, called Dracula in the Latin tongue, but Devil in the Russian language. He was evil but wise, of angry disposition, who did not pardon or spare anyone, and who punished evil by quick death.'

His conversion to Catholicism, his only deadly sin in the eyes of the Russians, was mitigated by the fact that, while a prisoner of King Matthias Corvinus of Hungary, far from his native land, he was confronted by a terrifying choice: either to embrace Catholicism and regain his throne or to rot in jail till his dying day. 'Dracula loved the sweetness of life temporal, rather than life endless and eternal, left his Pravoslav faith, and in giving up the Truth he lost the light and took on darkness. Alas, being unable to cope with the darkness and carry the burden of life temporal, and accepting eternal torture, he left our Pravoslav faith and embraced the rites of Catholicism. The [Hungarian] king not only returned to him the Mutyan lands but gave him his sister to be his wife.'

Although the monks who wrote the first two Dracula stories condemned the Walachian for forsaking the true Orthodox faith, they continued to regard him as a great ruler and defender of Christendom.

In order to facilitate the change in Dracula's character—from a mad torturer and butcher of innocents, as portrayed in the West, to a harsh but just autocratic ruler—the Russians only used six episodes from the original story. The eleven new ones that they included emphasised a ruler's God-given right to use torture and punish his subjects with cruelty if the common good so required.

That the Dracula story was being used as a moral code in Russia becomes quite evident if one compares the early German news-letters and the Russian *Povesty o Mutyanskom Voyevode Drakule*. In all German incunabula, Dracula has the Catholic monk who insincerely praises his oppressive rule impaled on a stake, while the monk who fearlessly denounces his cruelties is rewarded for his honesty. In the Russian version of the story the hypocritical monk is richly rewarded and the critic is instantly impaled.

The hypocritical monk of the Russian story explains the reason for this inversion of long-established European ethical values: 'God gave you, monarch, your power to punish wrong-doers and reward those doing good.' The inference is clear—the ruler is always right. As his power is of divine origin, his deeds cannot be judged by ordinary mortals. The Russian Dracula stories duly underline this basic tenet of Russian autocracy.

In the German news-letters Dracula punishes lazy women and kills his mistress because she displeases him by becoming pregnant. Sloth, apparently, was one of the less serious sins of Russian womanhood, however, and the Russian stories concentrate instead on castigating loose sexual morals. Erring wives who deceive their husbands have 'their sinful parts cut out' and are tied naked to a stake in the market place. Girls who lose their chastity and widows who break their marriage vows suffer the same fate. In the Russian story Dracula kills his mistress, not because she is pregnant but because she has lied to him.

Even the nailing of hats to ambassadorial heads, condemned in the German and other European Dracula stories as acts of a barbarian unversed in the usages of diplomacy, gains the approval of the Russian authors who saw it as the ruler's attempt to safeguard the authority of his state.

In another incident with a representative of a king [Matthias Corvinus of Hungary] more powerful than himself, Dracula forces the envoy to eat a hearty meal in a forest of impaled corpses under the shadow of a giant, unoccupied stake. Instead of having the envoy protest against the threat of impalement without reason the Russian version has him affirm that, no matter how cruelly he acts, the ruler is always right. 'Monarch! Should I have done anything that earned me the death sentence, do with me what you will', the envoy tells Dracula. 'For you are a just and true judge.'

The burning of the country's poor, condemned in the original German news-letters as an act of motiveless cruelty, also finds full justification in Russian. The *Povesty* presents it as Dracula's attempt to eradicate grinding poverty and earthly suffering. 'You must know', the Russian story has him say, 'why I'm doing it. First of all, so that they do not burden the people and to rid my country of the poor; and secondly to save them from the suffering, poverty and miseries of this world.'

The eradication of evil from the face of the earth at all costs was one of the popular justifications of autocratic power in Russia, and in the *Povesty* Dracula duly directs his attention to this moral problem, whereas in the German incunabula there is no mention of any such preoccupation. 'And hating to see evil on his land', the *Povesty* says of Dracula, 'none of those committing any evil, wickedness, highway robbery, or the telling of lies will he allow to live. Be he mighty boyar, or priest, or monk, or simpleton, or rich man, he cannot escape death, for so terrible was he.'

Thus there are very few unmotivated or gratuitous acts of cruelty in the Russian story, and occasionally Dracula even wins the open approval of the story's author. Between 1502 and the end of the seventeenth century twenty more versions of the Dracula story were written in Russia.* The great majority of the

* Together with the Kirilo-Byeloozerzsky and the Rumyantsev version there are altogether twenty-two known surviving versions, according to Y. S. Lurye, the Soviet Union's foremost Dracula researcher.

stories appeared during the reign of Ivan the Terrible, Ivan III's grandson,* to justify his tyranny and own pathological sadism.

Whereas Ivan III tortured and cruelly punished individual boyars whose feudal prerogatives interfered with the establishment of Muscovy's centralised power, his grandson sought altogether to end their feudal right to choose freely the liege master under whom they were to serve, and thereby destroy them as a *class*. To that end, large-scale butcherings were carried out by the Oprichniki, Ivan's secret police. The standard punishment meted out to heretics and opponents of the Autocrat's sacred power involved, in order to 'save their immortal soul, long spells of torture and eventual decapitation. Boyars who looked to Catholic Poland and Lithuania for support were skinned alive, grilled on charcoal under the personal supervision of the 'earthly representative of true Christianity', and thrown into the purifying waters of the icy Moskva river before being allowed to die an agonising death.

I. S. Peresvetov, a sixteenth-century apologist of Ivan the Terrible's psychotic sadism, defended his ruler's hair-raising acts on the ground that the Autocrat had a God-given right to judgment by torture. In his pamphlet *Bolshaya Chelobitnaya*† he wrote that the Tsar of all Russians must be cruel in order to fulfil his God-given task on earth, and punish his subjects without pity or control. Notions of natural justice were so qualified in his writings that in the end he claimed that 'justice cannot be established in the land without such terrors' (as perpetrated by the Tsar).

To what extent this tenet pervaded Russian national consciousness can be gauged from the treatise written by Ivan Volk Kurytsin, a Hussite sectarian and opponent of Muscovite Orthodoxy. Although challenging the 'divine' foundations of despotic Orthodoxy, he nevertheless accepted the Tsar's right to punish with cruelty and without regard for the fate of the individual.‡

* Ivan IV, called the Terrible, ruled from 1533 to 1584.
† A. A. Zimin: *I. S. Peresvetov i yego sovremenniki*, Moscow, 1958.
‡ Ivan Volk Kurytsin: *Merilo Pravednoye*, Moscow, a sixteenth century pamphlet.

The endeavour of the sixteenth century monastic authors of Russian Dracula stories to justify Ivan the Terrible's rule led eventually to the convergence of the two tyrannical figures. In the texts written in Ivan the Terrible's time and after his death, Dracula becomes the '*tsar grozny*'—the 'Terrible tsar'—and Muscovites begin to refer to Ivan the Terrible as 'the Russian Dracula.'

Even some of Dracula's deeds, such as the nailing of hats to ambassadorial heads, were attributed to Ivan the Terrible.

But as the political ideals expounded by the *Povesty* lost their immediate appeal to the Russians, who became bitterly disappointed by the failure of autocratic power to eradicate evil from their midst, the Dracula story was eclipsed. More and more folklore elements crept in and he lost virtually all his odious traits that qualified him for the 'Terrible Tsar' title in the previous century. In the Tikhonravov version of the *Povesty*, Dracula is already a positive hero, perfectly fit to inhabit the pages of edifying literary works.

By the time the Russian Romantic historian Karamzin came to examine the Dracula story in the nineteenth century, the Walachian 'hero' of the *Povesty* appeared to him as some sort of mythical figure expressing the fatalistic Russian adage that the only remedy against evil on earth is death.* The Dracula myth had really come into its own in Russia.

* N. M. Karamzin: *Istoriya gosudarstva Rossiyskogo*, Moscow, 1903.

SIXTEEN

Germany: Vampire Horror Fiction, Blood and the Nazi Myths

The Gothic horror tales of Victorian England, inspired by German ghost stories and haunted castles, reached their peak in Bram Stoker's *Dracula*. It was a late and unexpected flowering of the Gothic romance in a technologically advanced age. The revival of the ancient and indestructible myth of un-dead vampires re-awakened modern man's interest in the occult and in the super-natural at a time when science, the new religion, was rapidly pushing back the frontiers of the unknown.

The Transylvanian vampire and the myth of the un-dead returning from the grave to feast on human blood had fallen on fertile soil in Wilhelmin Germany. The eighteenth century ghost stories and tales of the macabre, which still had a vast following, were reinforced by *Dracula* and, in accordance with the laws of cross-fertilisation, produced a horror fiction with a difference. The vampire's predeliction for the blood of young females was greatly emphasised, lending the German stories a heavy sexual undertone. And the widespread preoccupation with Nordic myths and Teutonic blood rites, introduced into the vampire stories by the German practitioners of horror, gave the horror fiction an unexpected political significance.

The new generation of mystic nationalists, who found an elective affinity with Edgar Allen Poe's notably reactionary philosophy, welcomed Stoker's vampire as the consummate expression of the power of blood. To them, the drinking of human blood was not merely a rediscovery of the magic of forgotten Nordic rites, but also the realisation of the mystical Life Force.

Those returning from the grave were not frightening figures of horror, but superhuman *Übermenschen* heralding the destruction of the decadent old world and the creation of a New Order based on blood. The convergence of horror fiction and political literature in Germany lent the Dracula myth new dimensions.

The writings of Hans-Heinz Ewers reflect most clearly the close link between the blood-fixated mysticism of the literary precursors of National Socialism and the vampire Dracula conjured up by Bram Stoker. His life—from 1871 to 1943—spanned the high tide of German nationalism. His horror trilogy, completed around the First World War,* contained all the dark, shapeless Nordic mysticism and exultation of Teutonic blood rites that were to become so dear to the ideologists of the Nazi order. It also incorporated elements of barbarous cruelty—conspicuously missing from Stoker's horror fiction—which bear the hallmark of the historical Dracula. There is no incontrovertible proof that Ewers was acquainted with the Rennaissance German news-letters describing Vlad Dracula's horrible deeds but, during his researches into the ethnic origins of Rumanians and what he saw as the corruption of the once dominant Latin and Finno-Ugrian races, he could not have missed the Impaler.

On the eve of the First World War, Ewers became the most devoted and sympathetic interpreter of Poe's genius, but his eulogy of the American master of horrors was mixed with overtones of strident German nationalism.† In the first English

---

* *The Sorcerer's Apprentice*, 1910; *The Vampire*, 1921; *Nightmare*, 1922.

† In his essay *Edgar Allan Poe*, completed in 1916, Ewers wrote: 'He drank— he did not drink. That is the way the Anglo-Saxons dispute about their poets. They permit Milton to starve; they steal his whole life's work from Shakespeare. They delve into Byron's and Shelley's family histories with crooked fingers; they calumniate Rossetti and Swinburne; lock Wilde into prison and point their finger at Charles Lamb and Poe—because they drank!

'After all, I am happy that I am a German. Germany's great are permitted to be immoral—that is, not quite as moral as the good middle class and the priests. The German says: "Goethe was our great poet." He knows that he was not very moral but he does not take that fact too much to heart. The Englishman says: "Byron was immoral, therefore he cannot have been a great poet . . ."

'If, however, it is unalterable, if the nations on all sides acknowledge and love the "immoral" English poets, the Englishman is forced to speak—and then he lies. He does not renounce his hypocrisy; he simply says: "Later investigation

language publication of his essay★ on Poe he was, aptly enough, described as eminently suited 'to mirror the soul of Poe because they are intellectual kinsmen. Both are at home in the "misty mid-region of Weir", both dwell "out of Space, out of Time". Both have explored the realm of Horror. In fact, Ewers has gone beyond Poe because to him was revealed the mystery of sex.' Blood-crazed sex would, however, have been a more correct definition.

Indeed, Ewers went well beyond Poe—well beyond Stoker, too—in his conscious exploitation of the cruelty and blood-madness that had swept across Europe. The mystic aura and Teutonic fanaticism of his heroes spoke of the Valhalla, that special, reassuring corner of everlasting Germanic glory, and his horror tales provided defeated post-world war I Germany with the perfect escapism capable of thrilling and diverting the disillusioned masses.

At the same time, like, all other patriots, Ewers was dreaming of a new, Siegfried-like, Teutonic hero capable of reanimating a drained Germany and restoring her lost glory and national honour. Stoker's un-dead Dracula, sustained by the magic power of human blood, inspired Ewers in the creation of his vampire hero. The choice of the vampire Dracula as the model for his un-dead German hero was in part due to the Transylvanian's claim to be the representative of 'a conquering race' and Stoker's reference to Dracula's blood link with Attila the Hun. 'Here in the whirlpool of European races', says Stoker through his un-dead Dracula,' the Ugric tribes . . . found the Huns, whose warlike fury had swept the earth like a living flame, till the dying peoples held that in their veins ran the blood of those old witches who, expelled from Scythia, had mated with the devils in the desert. Fools, fools!

---

has proved that the man was not at all immoral, he was highly moral, quite pure and innocent" . . . The English are now permitted to appreciate Edgar Allan Poe, since it is officially attested that he was a highly moral being.

'But we, who make not the slightest claim to middle-class morality, we love him even if he drank. Yes, we love him even more because of his drink, because we know that just from this poison which destroyed his body *pure blossoms* shot forth, whose artistic worth is imperishable.'

★ H. H. Ewers: *Edgar Allan Poe*, New York, 1917.

What devil or what witch was ever so great as Attila, whose blood is in these veins?.'

The un-dead vampire with Hun blood in his veins, and endowed with all the Teutonic trappings of Wagnerian imagery, was, however, not conceived in a dream. It was born in the nightmare of defeated Germany. It haunted and thrilled Germany, and Ewers's two vampire books were vastly successful, as was *Nosferatu*,* a straight film version of the un-dead Transylvanian vampire.

In *The Vampire* and *Vampire's Prey*, Ewers also explored the netherworld of man's killer instincts. In his scheme of things, man's blood-fixation, like his yearning for supernatural powers, was all part of his heritage. The mystical potential of man's mind, when fully realised, could become the physical extension of his senses, transcending the limitations of the mortal body. In a strange and suggestive way his horror fiction contained the promise of an alternative existence.

This mystical approach to the nature of man's bloodthirstiness could also accommodate the newly emergent racialist theories of German nationalists. Ewers made the carrier of vampirism, 'this ancient affliction of mankind', a wandering Jewess, and extended the nightmare existence of bloodsuckers to become synonymous with life in decadent Europe. The German reincarnation of the Transylvanian vampire became the infected Everyman of the twentieth century, carrying blood-madness in his veins.

'The blood madness, it must have started somewhere, although we do not know where, but it is contagious and infects all the people who came into contact with it', Frank Braun, Ewers's un-dead Everyman in *The Vampire* tells Lotte Levi, the Jewish girl who has initiated him into blood-sucking. "They all want blood, blood, blood. Just as you did."

'She smiled a wan smile. "I know, my beloved. But do you think the millions of soldiers in Europe know more? They are unaware of their wild madness, of their thirst for blood—just as you were."

* *Nosferatu The Vampire*, a Prana Film, Berlin, 1922, directed by F. W. Murnaw.

' "But they don't want to drink blood, Lotte", he countered.

' "Are you so sure of that? Are you sure they don't? That none of them wanted to, not even wanted without realising it?"

' "I, too, dreamed of blood—of rivers of blood in which to drown our enemies! And that I grew above it I owe to you! The storm seized all the leaves and tossed them about near the ground, but it carried me high up into the clouds and beyond—up to the stars. Ask a hundred, a thousand, a million people, but not one of them will be able to tell you how it happened. They don't know because they were merely swept along by the storm. They saw red, all of them, as I did and you did. The time is red—red with blood, and in you it simply revealed itself more strongly, more divinely, if you like. Humanity had become stricken with a wild fever and had to drink blood to make themselves well and young again." '*

The mixture in the writings of Ewers of sacrilegious lust, excessive cruelty and the exultation of pre-Christian Germanic forms of worship greatly attracted the ideologists of the National Socialist party who were in search of a new religion. The attraction was mutual. The creator of the Vampire Everyman, too, appears to have delighted in the ancient magic of the Nazi symbol, the party's blood rites and worship of cruel Teutonic traditions.

Although the spiritual kinship between the Nazi belief in revival through bloodshed and Ewers's purification through the sacrifice of innocents is obvious, it must be said [in all fairness] that these themes were present in Ewers's writings long before the advent of Nazism in Germany. His belief in wild cruelty as a necessary means of bringing men of lower civilisations nearer to their god, expressed in 1911, sprang from the same mystic sense of nationalist superiority that nearly thirty years later justified the establishment of Nazi torture chambers and gas ovens. In *The Sorcerer's Apprentice*, written in the peace of Wilhelmin Germany, he also anticipated the Nazi holocaust:

'This rage of bloodthirsty madness, this sight of bloody, tormented sacrifices, this intoxication of strong wine, this fevered dancing and this restless, deafening music—by all such possible

* H. H. Ewers: *The Vampire*, New York, 1934.

means men drew and flung themselves into the depths, down to the last abysses, down to the original consciousness of the world, to the *blind will* that was its innermost being.'*

In *The Sorcerer's Apprentice* Ewers describes with great psychological realism the blood-crazed Devil Hunters of a small Italian mountain village out to exorcise the evil in their midst. The parallel with the exorcism of 'political evil' in the Germany of the 1930s by the blood-crazed stormtroopers of Hitler is just as evident as the close affinity between the hypnotic power Hitler came to hold over the German masses and the prophet's ability to stir up the Italian village and give it hope of purification through the sacrifice of an innocent maid. The girl, hypnotised into believing that she is a saint, eventually takes upon herself the sins of the world and is crucified.

While presaging the spirit of the Nazi New Order, the story also contains all the ingredients that assured through the centuries the survival of the Dracula myth. The possessed villagers in the book do not drink ordinary wine: their prophet's prayerful hands actually transform their drink into the Saviour's blood. Their frenzied fanaticism, the tortures in the hope of salvation, and the ritual sacrifice of innocents differ from the deeds of Vlad Dracula or Ivan the Terrible only in their politico-religious scope. The meaning attached to the blood rituals, together with the sadistic flagellations and the orgiastic communions, forms, however, an integral part of the new twentieth century Teutonic religion. The hysterical passage on the frenzied mass flaggellation and religious copulation of the Devil Hunters could have been taken, twenty or so years later, for a factual description of one of the storm trooper initiation rites:

'The saint pushed Carmelina over to the other three and took a heavy dog-whip from the wall. "Kneel down!" she commanded. "Bow your head to Earth and pray to the Lord".

'The four bodies were clean and polished, none bore traces of former scars and wounds. But the Lord's grace put such strength into the saint's weak arms that her blows were more fearful than those of the huge farmhand. In a few minutes the bodies were

* *The Sorcerer's Apprentice*, New York, 1927.

covered with blood, the skin burst and hung in shreds. The four writhed on the floor and cried and howled in their torment. In her desperate pain Carmelina plunged her teeth into the round shoulders of the Cornaro woman; but the latter embraced the lad with her fevered arm and dug her nails deep into his flesh. They writhed and twisted themselves into a confused knot, encircled each other with their arms and legs and steamed with blood and sweat. And repeatedly the saint's heavy whip whizzed down on the broken flesh.

'The prophet leaped up, faltered and staggered and fell down before Teresa [the saint]. "Beat me", he cried. And the whip curled in bloody stripes about his arms and chest . . . The Devil Hunters all crowded about, each desirous for the blessing of the whip. The saint's arm was unwearied. Every back received the blows of her scourge and it seemed as if the wounded flesh gleamed redder and that her stigmas were broader and stood out above all others.

'All the while she did not forget those whose bodies had been hitherto untouched. Ever again she called to the musicians: "Strip yourself, Silvia—come hither, Alessandro Riccioli". And it was as if her eyes gleamed more brightly over those whom no blood had yet defiled, as if her voice rejoiced more loudly when she covered these white, naked bodies with the moist red garment. And she did not grow weary. Ever weightier, ever more terrible fell her blows, as though she wanted to drown the hall in a sea of blood.'*

Ewers could no more lay the spirit he conjured up in 1911 than the sorcerer's apprentice of the fable could his. It led the creator of Germany's vampire saviour to Hitler's movement. The road to the Brown House was a straight one for Ewers, without moral impediments or ethical misgivings. Adolf Hitler's personal friendship helped Ewers in bridging the gap between horror fiction and Nazi political literature.

In 1932 he undertook to write the story of Horst Wessel, the SA leader killed in a street battle with the communists. Hitler saw the book as a committed piece of writing, capable of edifying

* H. H. Ewers: op. cit.

Germany's National Socialist youth. Ewers justified, both to himself and his great literary following, the writing of a Nazi propaganda book with one sentence: 'Horst Wessel had to die so that Germany could live.'

In an epilogue to *Horst Wessel*, dated September 15, 1932, he wrote: 'It is my pleasurable duty to thank all those who have helped me in the writing of this book. First and foremost I'd like to thank the Fuehrer of the German freedom movement— Adolf Hitler; for it was he who suggested a year ago in the Brown House that I should depict "the battle for the streets", to write a chapter of German history.'

After the consolidation of Nazi power, Hitler fell out with Ewers: he was put on the blacklist of forbidden authors, and his books were swept out of public libraries.* The German visionary of horror became an embarrassment to the Nazis. Even Ewers was out of space and out of time in the apocalytic reality of the Third Reich. Both the myth and its creator had outlived their usefulness, for Hitler was about to unleash another cycle of 'blood madness' which was to last for a thousand years. In the six years it lasted more blood was spilled than the master who had conjured up the German vampire monster could have dreamed of in all his nightmares.

* A decree issued by the Nazi Reichs Schrifttums Kammer put Ewers on 'The List of Harmful and Undesirable Authors' and ordered that 'all his works with the exception of *Horst Wessell* and *Reiter in Deutscher Nacht* be removed from libraries.

SEVENTEEN

USA: *Dracula and the Cold War*

No modern myth or work of fiction has rivalled the triumphal
march of the un-dead Transylvanian vampire through the newspapers, books, cinema screens and stages of the Anglo-Saxon
world. Bram Stoker's *Dracula* went through eleven editions in
Britain between 1897 and the beginning of the First World War,
and has sold over a million copies since. In the United States,
where Edgar Allan Poe's horror fiction has become part of the
folklore, it has not been out of print since it was first published
in 1899.

Hamilton Deane's stage adaptation of the book*—the first,
not counting Stoker's own ill-fated presentation of *Dracula, or
the Un-Dead* at the London Lyceum, on May 18, 1897, in order
to establish his copyright—was a fantastic success. First performed
in June, 1924 in Derby, the play was 'simply coining money', in
Deane's own words—'I could not go wrong with it, anywhere.'
This was no empty boast. In 1927, after touring Britain for three
years, he took the play to New York. With Bela Lugosi, a
Hungarian actor from Transylvania, in the title role, the pro-
duction became an instant Broadway success, and took America
and Canada by storm.

But it was the magic of Hollywood that made the greatest
contribution to the rapid spread of the Dracula myth. The
cinema had, in the years after the First World War, become not
only the most popular form of entertainment but also the medium

---

* The revised version of the play performed in the United States was written
by Deane and John L. Balderston, an American writer. *Dracula, the Vampire*, a
play in three acts, New York, 1927.

of mass communication. The success of the German silent film *Nosferatu* spurred on the Universal Picture Corporation to do a Dracula film, Hollywood style.

Deane's play, well adapted to the tastes of the Anglo-Saxon world, and Bela Lugosi's sinister, spine-chilling Dracula made Tod Browning's film, released in 1931, into a box-office success. 'Mr Lugosi succeeds in revealing the man-vampire as a hideous creature, one that few would like to encounter within the moss-covered walls of an old English abbey', wrote *The New York Times* cinema critic.

Lugosi himself explained the universal success of his Dracula performance and its terrifying lure for women throughout the world by his pet theory that 'women are interested in terror for the sake of terror. For generations they have been the subject sex. This seems to have bred a masochistic interest—an enjoyment of, or at least a keen interest in suffering, experienced vicariously through the screen.'*

That the women of America had found the vampire Dracula's magnetic power sexually attractive, and the horrifying repulsion emanating from his person irresistible, was borne out by Lugosi's vast fan mail. Ninety-seven per cent of those who put pen to paper to impart their emotional experiences while watching *Dracula* were women. Psychoanalysts of the Freudian school were quick to point out that the women who went to the cinema to be thrilled and frightened out of their wits were sexually frustrated, because 'morbid dread always signifies repressed sexual desires'.

But their somewhat simplistic dictum clearly did not apply to the vast cross-section of American society that fell under the spell of Dracula, or to the Ivy League élite who saw the vampire as the embodiment of the Faustian quest to conquer eternity.

On the whole, however, there was little attempt to read into the success of the Dracula story any intellectual motivation. The Dracula film and the host of other horror films subsequently marketed by Hollywood, were taken at face value and enjoyed as escapism from the ugly reality of the Depression.

Although there was no political faction, major writer or

* H. Ludlam: *The Life Story of Bram Stoker*, London, 1962.

American ideological movement in the 1930s to try to exploit the Dracula myth, the United States Army's psychological warfare division clearly recognised the hate appeal of the Transylvanian vampire. During the Second World War the vampire everyone loved to hate was linked to the traditionally cruel image of the Hun, providing the war effort with a most powerful weapon. Posters calling on Americans to fight against the Nazi hordes showed a Hun soldier with Drucala fangs dripping with the blood of innocents. This image, capable of arousing fear and righteous hatred at the same time, was not a sophisticated psychological weapon, but the immediacy of the image brought home to the masses what the war was all about with greater urgency than Roosevelt's fireside chats about the duty of the democracies to fight the evil of Nazism.

The extent to which the vampire Dracula had, in the public mind, been identified with the bloodthirsty Huns can be gauged from the decision of the United States Army to issue free paperback copies of Stoker's *Dracula* to the troops serving overseas.

These were, however, early days in the political exploitation of the Dracula myth in the United States. The Cold War issues, seen in America in stark moral terms of right and wrong, resulted in the ideologisation of the power conflict with the Soviet Union. In America's crusade against communism the crude image of a Russian soldier with Dracula fangs had no place. The battle for the mind of demoralised Europe became part of the wider fight America was waging as the defender of the free world and the western way of life, and the psychological weapons had to be chosen accordingly.

Russian bad faith in eastern Europe, the *putsch* in Czechoslovakia, the blockade of Berlin, the bloody purges and show trials, the rape of Hungary and the blatant subordination of the world communist movement to Russian national interests, provided America with ample ammunition. To fight communist subversion in America and western Europe was, in the eyes of James Forrestal and John Foster Dulles, as important as to counter Russian expansionism on a worldwide scale. But the red scare in the United States soon degenerated into the hysterical witch-hunt of the McCarthy era. In that fear and suspicion-ridden moral climate the Dracula story was rediscovered and used as a *parable of communist subversion*.

Count Dracula, it was argued by academics and politically-minded Californian psychologists, represents the expansionist forces of eastern Europe which seek to destroy, through violence and internal subversion, the democratic fabric of western civilisation. The count's interest in disorder and violence—the bogey of the law-abiding American citizen—was given special emphasis, and by way of proof it was pointed out that Jonathan Harker, Stoker's mouthpiece in the novel, had noted that the laws and customs of the West did not apply to Dracula's world.

The key to the political message of Stoker's book lay, it was claimed, in its symbolism. Interpreted in the right way, the Transylvanian's avowed intention to infiltrate England and establish a vampire colony capable of converting the whole population *to his way of life*, gained a thoroughly contemporary and most menacing meaning. Vampirism, if used as a code word for the demonic forces unleashed in modern man's psyche by the pressures of technological progress and social alienation, would indeed be a phenomenon free societies ought to take seriously. For against the political cunning and ruthless determination of the Transylvanian to achieve his secret purpose, Western man, lulled into false security by the living tradition and continuity of society, has virtually no defence. The threat posed to progress and Western civilisation by the fanatical hordes of the East is real, it was argued. And because of this false sense of security, even the conversion of the citizens of Europe's most rational and democratic state to vampirish political bloodlust would be far from impossible.

A brief treatise on the political significance of *Dracula*, published in the United States by Richard Wasson, an American redbrick don,* in the mid-1960s, is typical of the many attempts to read preconceived Cold War ideas into Bram Stoker's vampire theme. Although not memorable for its scholarship or depth of analysis,

* Richard Wasson: 'The politics of Dracula', *English Literature in Transition*, Vol. 9.

the essay is nonetheless of considerable interest because it reflects the realisation of the power of the Dracula myth in our time and offers an invaluable insight into its adaptation to Cold War purposes.

Wasson hardly hides his intention to turn the vampire Dracula theme into an ideologically loaded parable. For, as he notes, among the numerous psychological and sociological explanations of *Dracula's* success is the political theme of the novel 'which would appeal to audiences throughout the series of crises presented by the two world wars and the Cold War'. For those unversed in the language and symbolism of the period, he provides signposts and a pocket-size set of WASP Cold War values.

Dracula, of course, stands for the fanatical hordes of the East, and his vampirism represents the demonic forces of industrial strife and subversion. But he is confronted by a group of free men who resolve to thwart this evil plan. 'They see themselves as an alliance of free men, qualified by nationality, heredity or the possession of natural gifts.'

No Cold War parable would be complete without a reference to American military aid, and the character Quincy P. Morris, the archetypal Texas millionaire, provides the group 'with the necessary military aid, in the form of Winchesters'. Wasson also sees the comic American as the most pragmatic campaigner of the group. 'While Van Helsig is in charge of long-term plans, it is Morris who is always there with practical suggestions and who, on the spur of the moment, can make the best decisions,' he writes. 'Once, when the group is surprised by the Count, Morris concocts a plan of action which almost traps him. More importantly, when the Count is on the run and Van Helsig is directing his efforts to trap him, Morris points out that while the group is well prepared to exorcise evil spirits, they are virtually defenceless against more material threats from wolves and gypsy partisans. "I propose we add Winchesters to our armament. I have a kind of belief in a Winchester when there is any trouble." '*

Van Helsig, the only one to realise the true nature of the new pestilence brought into Britain by the Transylvanian, gains in political stature by his firm warning to those politically naive

* R. Wasson: op. cit.

liberals who want to treat this most dangerous social infection with traditional democratic remedies. ' "You are a clever man, friend John" ', Wasson quotes Van Helsig as telling Dr Seward, the psychologist, in Stoker's book. ' "You reason well and your wit is bold; but you are prejudiced. You do not let your eyes see nor your ears hear, and that which is outside your daily life is not of account to you. Do you not think that there are things which you cannot understand, and yet which are; that some people see things that others cannot?" ' The reasoning that justified the overruling of individual protests against the witch-hunt of the McCarthy era can be clearly discerned through the tendentious quotation. The Dracula myth was once again fused with an obnoxious form of state ideology.

The choice of Dracula's first victim—Lucy Westenra—gains, in Wasson's interpretation, a symbolic importance that Stoker could hardly have had in mind. Miss Westenra—the Light of the West—is 'a typical upper-middle-class Victorian woman who has known no evil', and the class content of the east European's decision to drain her of her blood first could hardly be overlooked.

In this Cold War parable, Miss Westernra stands for the defenceless people of Christian Europe who, because of their lack of political guile, are the easy prey of east European agitators. Madam Mina Harker, on the other hand, displays all the moral strength that free people show in adversity. She too gets bitten by the vampire, 'but instead of deserting to the Count, she uses her new-found sympathy with his un-British east European habits to help the allies track him down.'*

The madman Renfield is used as a proof that, although the Transylvanian can manipulate certain elements of Western society, the moral steadfastness of men born free is in the end stronger than the potent spiritual poison of the communist East. 'Renfield, unlike the Eastern European Count, recognises the horror of his dream. He has himself committed, and though it costs him his life, he resists the Count's bribes . . . in order to warn the others of Dracula's strategy. English reason is strong enough to counter eastern European bloodlust, even in a lunatic.'†

* R. Wasson: op. cit.   † R. Wasson: op. cit.

In the end the allies prove that, although social and scientific progress make the Western world vulnerable, the very same forces can provide the means by which Dracula's threat to social stability can be laid. They are men unfettered by dogma who have both the resources of science and the free will to use them. The Austrian, as Wasson insists on calling Stoker's Dracula, is limited by the narrowness of his purpose, has not got freedom of movement and can convert only those who show willingness to cooperate with him. In a word, he is hampered in the subversion of the West by his own lack of freedom. Exploiting this Achilles heel of the communists, the allies, under the protective cover of American Winchesters, go into a counter-attack and finish off this menacing East European spectre in his own lair.

The parable ends on a hopeful note: 'The Count is controverted (sic) and his threat to the progress of Western civilisation is brought to an end. While on the surface Stoker's Gothic political romance affirms the progressive aspects of English and Western society, its final effect is to warn the twentieth century of the dangers which faced it, both in the years following Dracula's publication and in the present . . . The popular imagination so stirred by the political horrors of our time, which turns again and again to the nightmares of the Nazi era and which reads the warnings of science fiction with great attention, cannot help but be stirred by the political implications of Dracula.'*

American society for one appears to be tiring of both the Cold War and its myth-makers. But the Dracula myth lives on.

EPILOGUE

Amid the endless and often violent changes in the spiritual make-up of European civilisation in the past five centuries, the mass appeal of the Dracula myth, like a weathervane indicating the direction of the prevalent social winds, has remained astonishingly constant.

In differing societies fired by diametrically opposed political ideals the myth has been embroidered and endowed with greatly disparate meanings, now one, now the other of its basic components receiving special emphasis. The central European rulers who used Dracula's deeds to justify the establishment of absolute monarchies have long since disappeared from the political arena, together with their once mighty empires. The Russian despots and German supermen, who made the myth an important strand in the cultural weave of their societies, have been obliterated. And the crusading churches which found the scare engendered by some aspects of the myth useful in their dogmatic sparrings have fallen on hard times in eastern Europe. But Dracula lives on, with his myth duly reflecting the different development of East and West: in central and western Europe the un-dead Transylvanian goes on thrilling the masses with his blood-sucking act, whereas in the East Dracula is invoked as the epitome of the just but harsh defender of the state.

Modern man's preoccupation with the supernatural cannot alone explain the undiminished appeal of the vampire Dracula in our atomic age. The myth, successfully blending innocent yearnings with dark killer instincts that still course through the deep subterranean passages of the human psyche, also provides a touch of magic in a world denuded of romance. It is a magic all the more powerful because it transcends the limitations imposed by science and the soul-killing routine of life in suburbia. It is an escape from earth-bound materialism.

The increased appetite for horror, experienced vicariously from the safety of a cinema seat or the armchair comfort of the sitting-room, has indeed been one of the striking features of the post-war affluent society. It has led to a veritable renaissance of the horror film industry, centred around Dracula and Frankenstein. But for the cinema audiences of the 1950s and the television viewers of the 1960s Lugosi's money-spinning 1931 *Dracula*, reissued in 1938 and 1948, and such Hollywood 'classics' as *The Mark of the Vampire*, *The Return of the Vampire* and *The House of Dracula*, had lost something of their horrifying and haunting effect.

Then Hammer Films of London came up with a new formula of violence, torture and sensual blood-sucking, and horror fans, hoping for an ample flow of blood, flocked in their millions to see these films, at a time when the film industry as a whole was going through its worst crisis. Hammer's *Dracula* (1958), with Christopher Lee and Peter Cushing in the main roles, succeeded in bringing up to date the ancient Transylvanian horrors. With the inimitable Mr Lee as the vampire with British sang-froid, Hammer Films produced in quick succession a battalion of Dracula films for world-wide distribution.* Their hallmark was the way they lingered on the disagreeable physical aspects of the theme, leaving virtually nothing to the imagination.

Film-makers the world over were quick to realise the mass appeal of horror films, and by mixing bloodlust with sex greatly extended the commercial exploitation of the vampire myth. Le Fanu's *Carmilla* was recreated, with considerable licence, in *The Vampire Lovers*, loading sex, lesbianism and vampirism unto a nineteenth-century Gothic romance.

Many variations on the theme followed, and lesbian vampirism has recently become the staple horror diet. A throw-away line from my researches into Countess Elisabeth Báthory's acts was spun out and converted into a full-length period film under the alluring title of *Countess Dracula*.† A weird surrealistic fantasy,

* The more successful ones, dubbed 'screamies', included *The Brides of Dracula*, *Taste the Blood of Dracula*, *Dracula has Risen from the Grave*, *The Scars of Dracula*, and *Dracula—Prince of Darkness*.

† *Countess Dracula*, produced by Alexander Paal, directed by Peter Sasdy, 1971.

the *Daughter of Darkness*,* in which Countess Elisabeth Báthory and her perverted accomplice, Ilona, batten onto a newly-wed couple on their honeymoon, succeeded rather better in conveying the essence of the vampire horror. Shot in a showy baroque manner, the film at least softened the scenes of murder and blood-sucking with techniques borrowed from *L'année dernière à Marienbad*.

Others explored the world of science-gone-mad and produced a horror fiction much more suited to our reality. The master-pieces of Poe, Mary Shelley and Wells were re-made to suit popular tastes, and the themes provided by them were thickly padded out with realistic details capable of sending shivers down the spines of men living in the shadow of a nuclear holocaust.

All these were real horror films, without the benefit of poetry or the quaint hauntings of the first Dracula films. But they broke all previous box-office records and, in recognition of the foreign exchange earnings of their screamies, Hammer Films were presented with the Queen's Award to Industry for Export Achievement in 1968. Mr Lee, who did perhaps more than anyone else to perpetuate the Transylvanian horror as a commercial way of life, was received in audience by the Queen.

Those who feared that the new horror cult was an expression of a deep-running social sickness began to sound the moral alarm bells in the mass media of the Western world. The genre which, however morbidly, describes actions exceedingly far removed from the everyday experiences and environment of the audiences, was once again scrutinised by men and women with a social conscience.

Such sociologists and political journalists, their horizon darkened by Freud's 'Uncanny', saw the vampire Dracula films as an invitation to sessions of collective sadism and cruelty. Others denounced the commercial exploitation of the streak of violence and cruelty which linger in man's subconscious. Hints that the continued success of the vampire Dracula and Mary

* *Daughters of Darkness*, directed by Peter Kumel, 1971.

Shelley's monster was a clear expression of social alienation and a revolt against the materialism of the affluent society abounded. But the politically-motivated inspiration of the analyses precluded a more positive approach to the Dracula myth which has fascinated and sickened, incensed and at the same time thrilled, countless generations.

Man does not live by bread alone, and his need to believe in a creed, a leader or a religion that can justify his existence is only surpassed by his myth-making ability. The survival of the myths attaching to Vlad Dracula is as good an example of this as any in European history. In his own homeland, Rumania, Vlad Dracula lives on as a harsh but just ruler, always ready to aid his people in a national emergency. Nations, like people, have a selective memory. Vlad Dracula's unspeakable cruelties, the forests of impaled corpses and his delight in the prolonged agony of his innocent victims, have fallen through the sieve of national consciousness. The Impaler's cruelty, one is told, was directed against the Turks, the Hungarians and the Germans. He protected the forebears of the present Rumanian nation, and excess in the defence of freedom—in the words of a twentieth century myth-maker*—is a virtue rather than a sin. Vlad Dracula, the Impaler, also dispensed a kind of mediaeval rough justice, assuring law and order in his country, and cutting petty tyrants down to size, something that appeals to modern man, bossed and ordered about by a well-nigh intolerable bureaucracy. From a distance of some five centuries, Vlad Dracula is a ruler clad in the shining armour of a national saviour.

The Rumanians are not alone either in having a selective corporate memory, or in their myth-making. Ask a law-abiding middleaged German and he will say that Hitler might have made mistakes but he ended unemployment and built the autobahns. Mussolini might have been a trifle vain and precipitate, but he made the trains run on time. The Russians, who lost more people in Stalin's senseless purges and as a result of his readiness to pay any price for industrialisation than they had in the Second World War, are beginning to remember the dictator as the great builder

*John F. Kennedy.

of socialism. The Americans are no exception: the brief period of President Kennedy's rule is already looked upon as a golden era of national greatness and stylish government. Man can no more live without myths than without air.

Index